PROVERBS

from

AROUND THE WORLD'

1500 amusing, witty and
insightful proverbs from
21 lands and languages

PROVERBS

from

AROUND THE WORLD

1500 amusing, witty and
insightful proverbs from
21 lands and languages

by

Norma Gleason

A Citadel Press Book
Published by Carol Publishing Group

Carol Publishing Group Edition, 1995

A Citadel Press Book
Published by Carol Publishing Group
Citadel Press is a registered trademark of Carol Communications, Inc.

Editorial Offices: 600 Madison Avenue, New York, NY 10022
Sales & Distribution Offices: 120 Enterprise Avenue, Secaucus, NJ 07094
In Canada: Canadian Manda Group, One Atlantic Avenue, Suite 105
Toronto, Ontario, M6K 3E7

Queries regarding rights and permissions should be addressed to:
Carol Publishing Group, 600 Madison Avenue, New York, NY 10022

Carol Publishing Group books are available at special discounts
for bulk purchases, sales promotions, fund raising, or
educational purposes. Special editions can also be created to
specifications. For details contact: Special Sales Department,
Carol Publishing Group, 120 Enterprise Ave., Secaucus, NJ 07094

Manufactured in the United States of America
10 9 8 7 6 5 4 3 2

Illustrations:

© Dover Publications, PICTORIAL ARCHIVE OF DECORATIVE AND ILLUSTRATIVE MORTISED CUTS, edited by Carol Belanger Grafton

© Dover Publication, OLD-FASHIONED MORTISED CUTS, edited by Carol Belanger Grafton

Library of Congress Cataloging-in-Publication Data

Proverbs from around the world : 1500 amusing, witty, and insightful
    proverbs from 21 lands and languages / [compiled] by Norma Gleason.
        p.   cm.
    "A Citadel Press book."
    ISBN 0-8065-1310-1
    1. Proverbs. I. Gleason, Norma
PN6405.P72   1992
398.9—dc20   92-8869
                                              CIP

Contents

Advice 5
Age 5
Attitudes 6
Authority 8

Beauty 11
Beggars 11
Behavior 12
Belief 14
Books 14

Caution 17
Character 19
Children 20
Common Sense 22
Companions 22
Competence 23
Confidence 24
Conscience 24
Consequences 24
Contentment 26
Cooperation 27

Death 31
Desperation 32
Destiny 32

Differences   33
Drink   33

Envy   39
Equality   39
Error   40
Excuses   40
Experience   41

Faults and Virtues   45
Finality   45
Fools   46
Foolishness   48
Friends and Enemies   49
Futile Expectations   51

Good and Evil   55
Greed   56
Guests   56

Habit   61
Health   61
Hindsight   62
Hunger   62

Impossibilities   67
Industry and Sloth   68
Ingratitude   69

Judgement   73
Justice and Injustice   73

Laws   77
Love   77

Marriage   83
Misfortune and Fortune   84
Money   87

Patience 93
Persistence 93
Poverty 94
Preferable Alternatives 95
Prematurity 96
Pride 96

Quarrels 101

Rationalization 105
Reality 105
Relativity 106
Religion 107
Resignation 108

Secrecy 111
Sequences 111
Speech 112
Superfluity 113
Superiority 114
Suspicion 114

Teachers 117
Thrift and Prudence 117
Timeliness 118
Travel 119
Truth and Falsehood 120

Useless Pursuits 125

Value 129
Vanity 129

Weeping 133
Wisdom 133
Wishful Thinking 135

Introduction

Collecting proverbs for this book was both fun and educational. I discovered that through proverbs, every language reveals the unique attitudes and culture of its people. French proverbs, I found, tend to be philosophical and intellectual, as with "If the triangles had a god, they would give him three sides." Irish and Scottish proverbs embody a caustic wit: "Ye come from the McTakes, but not from the McGives" (Scottish). And Russian proverbs show a stoic acceptance of whatever fate deals out: "If there is no apple, one eats a little carrot."

Although, as a rule, the line between quotations and proverbs is distinct, it is not so easy to distinguish among old sayings, proverbs and certain quotations that have passed into the sphere of proverb lore, such as Benjamin Franklin's "A word to the wise is sufficient." A few proverbs in this book may be classified by some scholars as proverbs and by other scholars as old sayings.

Proverbs travel from country to country. The Spanish say "En tierra de ciegos, el tuerto es rey." The French express the same thought in their own language, as we do when we say in English, "In the land of the blind, the one-eyed is king."

Or the same thought is expressed in totally different words, reflecting differing lifestyles. English-speaking peoples say "Give him an inch and he'll take a mile." The Arab version of this philosophy is "Let the camel get his nose in the tent and the body will soon follow."

Proverbs often deal with man's disillusionment with his lot. An Arab may wail, "If I sold winding sheets, no one would die," and a Spaniard complain, "I wept when I was born, and every day explains why."

For the convenience of writers and speakers, the proverbs are sorted out into categories from *Advice* to *Wishful Thinking*. Under each category heading the proverbs are listed alphabetically by origin.

May you enjoy browsing among these proverbs as much as I have enjoyed collecting them.

ACKNOWLEDGMENTS

I owe special thanks to Gene DeGruson, Special Collections Librarian of the E. Haldeman-Julius collection at the Leonard H. Axe library at Pittsburg (Kansas) State University. Mr. DeGrusen kindly provided me with photocopies of the little proverb books from his collection, first published forty and fifty years ago.

I am also indebted to Dr. Leo Hamlian of Ararat Press, Saddle Brook, New Jersey, for permission to use Armenian proverbs from their book "Seven Bites from a Raisin"; and to Dr. Kermit Westbrook of Augustana College, Rock Island, Illinois for providing me with hard-to-find Swedish proverbs from their private collection.

Last but not least I need to thank John and Elaine Gill of The Crossing Press for permission to use proverbs from "The Proverb Book."

I have also taken the liberty of judiciously borrowing a few proverbs here and there from other large published volumes and express gratitude for these borrowings. They constitute a minor portion of the 1500 proverbs.

Norma Gleason

A

I gave so much
advice that hair
grew on my
tongue.
Persian

Advice
Age
Attitudes
Authority

Advice

1. Advice given in the midst of a crowd is loathsome. *Arab*
2. When the cart breaks down, advice is plentiful. *Armenian*
3. Nobody will give a pauper bread, but everybody will give him advice. *Armenian*
4. If I had given fourpence for the advice, I bought it a groat too dear. *English*
5. We should never be ashamed to take advice, even from the lowly. *German*
6. Don't give cherries to pigs, nor advice to fools. *Irish*
7. He is bad that will not take advice, but he is a thousand times worse who takes every advice. *Irish*
8. Do not give advice unless you have the wisdom to go with it. *Irish*
9. Teeth placed before the tongue give good advice. *Italian*
10. Himself in disgrace, he gives others free advice. *Persian*
11. I gave so much advice that hair grew on my tongue. *Persian*
12. The wise must be respected, even when the advice they give us is not suitable. *Sanskrit*
13. A woman's advice is of little value, but he who does not take it is a fool. *Spanish*

Age

14. To succeed, consult three old people. *Chinese*
15. Don't laugh at age . . . pray to reach it. *Chinese*
16. Every age wants its playthings. *French*
17. When we are old, all our pleasures are behind us, but when we are young, all our troubles are before us. *Irish*
18. When a lion is old, he becomes the plaything of jackals. *Persian*

19. At twenty a man will be a peacock, at thirty a lion, at forty a camel, at fifty a serpent, at sixty a dog, at seventy a monkey and at eighty nothing. *Spanish*
20. The young should be taught, the old should be honored. *Swedish*
21. A man shows in his youth what he will be in his age. *Yugoslav*

Attitudes

22. On the day of victory no one is tired. *Arab*
23. Clothes when new make you swagger, when old make you ashamed. *Arab*
24. Do not ridicule the thin-bearded when you yourself have no beard. *Arab*
25. Can one start a fast with baklava in one's hand? *Armenian*
26. Let everyone sweep away the snow from his own door, and not meddle with the hoarfrost on his neighbor's tiles. *Chinese*
27. A man who cannot tolerate small ills can never accomplish great things. *Chinese*
28. The thief is sorry that he is to be hanged, not that he is a thief. *English*
29. People who live in glass houses shouldn't throw stones. *English*
30. There are none so deaf as those that won't hear. *English*
31. In the land of the blind, the one-eyed is king. *French*
32. The first half of life is spent in longing for the second, the second half in regretting the first. *French*
33. The most wasted of all days is the day when we have not laughed. *French*
34. A man is no happier than he thinks himself. *French*
35. If you cannot catch a fish, do not blame the sea. *Greek*
36. The fox that had her tail cut off tried to entice the others to imitate her. *Greek*
37. If you call a lady a slave, she laughs, but if you call a slave a slave, she cries. *Hindustan*
38. He that has a jaundiced eye sees everything yellow. *India*

39. Is it necessary to add acid to the lemon? *India*
40. The pot broken by the mother-in-law was a cracked pot; the pot broken by the daughter-in-law was a new pot. *India*
41. It avails nothing to be offended by the arrow instead of the archer. *India*
42. He does not see the speck in his own eye, but stares at the mote in another's. *India*
43. All the turf in the bog wouldn't warm me to him. *Irish*
44. The heaviest ear of corn is the one with its head bent low. *Irish*
45. A burden which one chooses is not felt. *Italian*
46. The would-be buyer always depreciates. *Italian*
47. A man with a sour face should not open a shop. *Japanese*
48. If a man is poor and humble, even his wife and children will despise him; if he is rich and powerful, even the folk of far-off countries will praise him. *Japanese*
49. Cold rice and cold tea are bearable, but cold looks and cold words are not. *Japanese*
50. By one ear he hears, and by the other he dismisses. *Persian*
51. The shovel insults the poker. *Russian*
52. It will last out our time; if after us no grass grows, what does it matter to us? *Russian*
53. To ask is no sin, and to be refused is no calamity. *Russian*
54. If a man's heart be impure, all things will appear hostile to him. *Sanskrit*
55. It is not the fault of the post that a blind man cannot see it. *Sanskrit*
56. They know not their own defects who search for the defects of others. *Sanskrit*
57. The tree that is cut down grows again; the moon that wanes after a time waxes again. Thus do wise men reflect and, though distressed, are not overwhelmed. *Sanskrit*
58. He that has a big nose thinks everyone speaks of it. *Scottish*
59. If I die, I forgive you; if I recover, we shall see. *Spanish*
60. The good man cannot always escape calumny. *Spanish*
61. What matter if I suffer, if only my neighbor suffers too. *Swedish*

62. We should think and speak well of each other. *Swedish*
63. If you would call the dog to you, do not carry a stick. *West Africa*
64. The sparrow says, "I did not eat, therefore the parrot should not eat." *West Africa*
65. There is no medicine to cure hatred. *West Africa*
66. A bowl should not laugh when a calabash breaks. *West Africa*
67. When one is not good oneself, one likes to talk of what is wrong with others. *Yugoslav*
68. It is better to look from the mountain than from the dungeon. *Yugoslav*

Authority

69. Authority brooks no partner. *French*
70. The strong obey when the stronger order. *Irish*
71. The horse may wish to do one thing, but he who saddles him another. *Spanish*
72. Who gives the bread lays down the authority. *Spanish*
73. Permission is needless to him who has the power to take without it. *Spanish*
74. It is pleasant to command, be it only a herd of cattle. *Spanish*
75. Where the water rules, the land submits. *West Africa*
76. When the big bells ring, the little bells are not heard. *Yugoslav*
77. He who does not know how to serve cannot know how to command. *Yugoslav*
78. If you wish to know what a man is, place him in authority. *Yugoslav*

B

Beauty
without grace
is as a rose
without scent.
Swedish

Beauty
Beggars
Behavior
Belief
Books

Beauty

79. Beauty is power. *Arab*
80. Though the peony be beautiful, it must be supported by green leaves. *Chinese*
81. Handsome is as handsome does. *English*
82. Beauty is only skin deep. *English*
83. Beauty is the eye's food but the soul's sorrow. *German*
84. What does the blind man know of the beauty of the tulip? *Hindustan*
85. Beauty does not make the pot boil. *Irish*
86. Beauty is only skin deep, but nobody wants to be drowned. *Irish*
87. What worth has beauty if it not be seen? *Italian*
88. Is there anything naturally beautiful or not beautiful? Whatever is pleasing to anyone, that is beautiful for him. *Sanskrit*
89. The voice is the beauty of cuckoos; chastity is the beauty of women; learning is the beauty of the deformed; patience is the beauty of ascetics. *Sanskrit*
90. Lovely flowers fade fast. Weeds last the season. *Swedish*
91. Beauty without grace is as a rose without scent. *Swedish*
92. A chicken with beautiful plumage does not sit in a corner. *West Africa*

Beggars

93. If begging should unfortunately be your lot, knock at the large gates only. *Arab*
94. If wishes were horses, then beggars could ride. *English*
95. Beggars can't be choosers. *English*

96. A beggar on his feet is worth more than an emperor in his grave. *French*
97. Though you are going begging, go decently attired. *India*
98. He is a beggar, but he demands sweetmeats as alms. *India*
99. If a beggar be placed in the midst of a grove of pear trees, even there he will beg. *India*
100. Constant begging means constant refusal. *Irish*
101. A beggar must be prepared to wait. *West Africa*
102. A beggar won't mind being insulted. *West Africa*
103. The best morsels are never given to a beggar. *West Africa*

Behavior

104. When the market is brisk, the seller does not stop to wash the mud from his turnips. *Chinese*
105. There is no one to sweep a common hall. *Chinese*
106. If you bow at all, bow low. *Chinese*
107. Some have been thought brave because they were afraid to run away. *English*
108. Charity begins at home. *English*
109. Ye be as full of good manners as an egg be of oatmeal. *English*
110. From a short pleasure comes a long repentance. *French*
111. Let everyone carry his own sack to the mill. *German*
112. Spur not a willing horse. *German*
113. It is little honor to the lion to seize the mouse. *German*
114. When you go to bed with a clear head, you will never rise with a headache. *Greek*
115. If you are a priest, be a priest; if you are a plowman, be a plowman. *Greek*
116. Dependence on another is perpetual disappointment. *Hindustan*
117. The sieve with a thousand holes finds fault with the basket. *India*
118. Who will pay for the shoe of a partnership horse? *India*

119. It is easy to forget a kindness, but one remembers unkindness. *India*
120. It is not for the blind to give an opinion on colors. *Italian*
121. Do not prophesy to the man who can see further than you can. *Japanese*
122. He cries before he is beaten. *Persian*
123. Be bad to the bad and good to the good; be a flower unto a flower and a thorn unto a thorn. *Persian*
124. Make thyself a sheep and the wolf is ready. *Russian*
125. Should a peasant become a landlord, he will flay the peasants. *Russian*
126. If men could foresee the future, they would still behave as they do now. *Russian*
127. Do not spit into the well—you may have to drink out of it. *Russian*
128. Ye have good manners, but ye don't carry them about with ye. *Scottish*
129. An ill-tempered question deserves an ill-tempered answer. *Scottish*
130. Lock your door and preserve your neighbor's honor. *Spanish*
131. She alone is chaste who has never been sought. *Spanish*
132. Kindness begets kindness. *Swedish*
133. Fear less, hope more. Eat less, chew more. Sigh less, breathe more. Hate less, love more, and all good things are yours. *Swedish*
134. When you are among the blind, shut your eyes. *Turkish*
135. At meal time, "Yes!" When duty calls, "No!" *West Africa*
136. Why pucker up your lips when you have no intention to weep? *West Africa*
137. He who picks up a thorn on the road has one less sin, for had he stepped on it, he would have cursed. *Yugoslav*
138. Condemn a man within his hearing; praise him when he is away. *Yugoslav*
139. He who humbles himself too much gets trampled upon. *Yugoslav.*

Belief

140. There are no miracles to the man who does not believe in them. *French*
141. To believe everything is too much, to believe nothing is not enough. *German*
142. Don't believe everything you hear nor tell all that you know. *Italian*
143. The more one knows, the less one believes. *Italian*
144. Believe all ye hear and ye may eat all ye see. *Scottish*
145. Of what you see, believe very little, of what you are told, nothing. *Spanish*

Books

146. You cannot open a book without learning something. *Chinese*
147. Every book must be chewed to get out its juice. *Chinese*
148. God deliver me from a man of one book. *English*
149. Every abridgment of a good book is a stupid abridgment. *French*
150. It is of no use to have the book without the learning. *Irish*
151. A book, to a blind man, signifies nothing. *Irish*
152. He who lends a book, one of his hands should be cut off. He who returns it, both his hands should be cut off. *Persian*

C

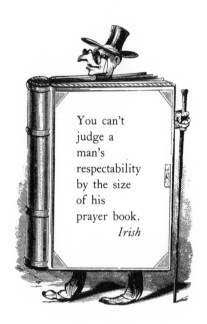

You can't
judge a
man's
respectability
by the size
of his
prayer book.
Irish

Caution
Character
Children
Common Sense
Companions
Competence

Confidence
Conscience
Consequences
Contentment
Cooperation

Caution

153. The dry reed does not seek the company of the fire.　*Arab*
154. Caution secures not cowards from death; it comes from the sky.　*Arab*
155. The chameleon does not leave one tree until he is sure of another.　*Arab*
156. Do not stand in a place of danger trusting in miracles.　*Arab*
157. The mouse that has but one hole is soon caught.　*Arab*
158. Don't pour away the water you are traveling with because of a mirage.　*Arab*
159. Do not drink poison thinking you can rely on the antidote you possess.　*Arab*
160. While the cautious one ponders, the fool will cross the bridge. *Armenian*
161. He who was bitten by a snake avoids tall grass.　*Chinese*
162. Before you beat the dog, learn the name of his master.　*Chinese*
163. The burnt child dreads the fire.　*English*
164. When in doubt, do nothing.　*English*
165. Look before you leap.　*English*
166. Little boats must keep the shore, larger boats may venture more.　*English*
167. Forewarned is forearmed.　*English*
168. Don't buy a pig in a poke.　*English*
169. He who has burned his tongue does not forget to blow on the soup.　*German*
170. A flatterer has water in one hand and fire in the other. *German*
171. Do not lean on a worm-eaten staff.　*Greek*
172. He who has been scalded with hot milk blows even on butter-milk before he drinks it.　*Hindustan*

173. Though the snake be small, it is wise to hit it with a big stick. *India*
174. Look at the wind before you let loose the boat. *India*
175. Never put your hand out further than you can draw it back again. *Irish*
176. Don't throw away the sweepings in the bag until you see did you drop your ring into it? *Irish*
177. The best armor is to keep out of gunshot. *Italian*
178. The stitch is lost unless the thread is knotted. *Italian*
179. By poking at a bamboo thicket, you may drive out a snake. *Japanese*
180. Trust in God, but tie your camel. *Persian*
181. If a man knew where he would fall, he would spread a carpet first. *Russian*
182. Look before ye leap and ye'll ken better how to light. *Scottish*
183. The blind man's peck should be well measured. *Scottish*
184. If ye cannot see the bottom, do not wade far out. *Scottish*
185. It's good to be civil, as the old wife said when she beckoned to the devil. *Scottish*
186. When the cup is full, carry it even. *Scottish*
187. It is better that they say "Here he ran away," than "Here he died." *Spanish*
188. The scalded cat flees even from cold water. *Spanish*
189. In large rivers one finds big fish but one may also be drowned. *Spanish*
190. Don't wake up sleeping sadness. *Swedish*
191. Measure forty times, cut once. *Turkish*
192. Do not step on the tail of a sleeping dog. *Turkish*
193. The lamb that strays from the field will be eaten by the wolf. *Turkish*
194. Who was once bitten by a snake fears a twisted rope. *Turkish*
195. He who has been bitten by a snake avoids the tall grass. *Yugoslav*
196. No one likes to be the first to step on ice. *Yugoslav*

Character

197. Better to lose your eye than your good name. *Armenian*
198. If your beard were on fire, he'd light his cigarette on it. *Armenian*
199. It is better to do a kindness near home than go far to burn incense. *Chinese*
200. To save one man's life is better than to build a many-storied pagoda. *Chinese*
201. If you are standing upright, do not fear a crooked shadow. *Chinese*
202. Still waters run deep. *English*
203. It is a double pleasure to deceive the deceiver. *French*
204. Talent is born in silence but character is born in the struggle of life. *German*
205. He who holds the ladder is as bad as the thief. *German*
206. He who goes unpunished never learns. *Greek*
207. Self-deceit is fate's saddest irony. *Greek*
208. A snake will emit only poison even though you feed it on milk. *India*
209. What you give wouldn't blind the eye of a midge. *Irish*
210. He would cover a rock with hay and sell it for a haystack. *Irish*
211. A fair character is a fair fortune. *Irish*
212. He'd give you an egg if you promised not to break the shell. *Irish*
213. You can't judge a man's respectability by the size of his prayer book. *Irish*
214. If better were within, better would emerge. *Irish*
215. He is so stingy that if he gave you the measles, it would be one measle at a time. *Irish*
216. She's about as honest as a basket is watertight. *Irish*
217. Titles do not make men illustrious; men make their titles illustrious. *Italian*
218. Of two cowards, the one who finds the other out first has the advantage. *Italian*

219. Even if you put a snake in a bamboo tube, you cannot change its wriggling disposition. *Japanese*
220. Look the other way when the girl at the teahouse smiles. *Japanese*
221. A man's good name is as precious to him as its skin is to a tiger. *Japanese*
222. A good reputation sits still, a bad one runs about. *Russian*
223. Fortune attends the man who exerts himself. They are weak who declare fate the sole cause. *Sanskrit*
224. Inactivity from fear of committing a fault is the mark of a coward. By whom is food renounced for fear of indigestion? *Sanskrit*
225. Ye come from the McTakes but not from the McGives. *Scottish*
226. They are free with their horse who have none. *Scottish*
227. He's worth no well that can bide no woe. *Scottish*
228. Faces we see, hearts we know not. *Spanish*
229. Honor is the throne of integrity. *Spanish*
230. If guilt were a robe of sable nobody would wear it. *Turkish*
231. If he were rain he would not fall on your field. *Turkish*
232. Where there is no shame, there is no honor. *West Africa*
233. If you refuse to be made straight when you are green, you will not be made straight when you are dry. *West Africa*
234. He is not honest who has burned his tongue and does not tell the company the soup is hot. *Yugoslav*

Children

235. To understand your parent's love, bear your own children. *Chinese*
236. The same tree may bear sweet and sour fruit; the same mother may have clever and stupid children. *Chinese*
237. A growing youth has a wolf in his stomach. *English*
238. Children should be seen and not heard. *English*

239. Spare the rod and spoil the child. *English*
240. Little pitchers have big ears. *English*
241. He that has no children does bring them up well. *English*
242. One father can support twelve children, but twelve children cannot support one father. *French*
243. In the young, silence is better than speech. *Greek*
244. Your dog and your child act as you teach them. *Greek*
245. Rear and nourish children with kindness, but chastise with severity. *Hindustan*
246. The baby is not yet born, and yet you say that his nose is like his grandfather's. *India.*
247. Bricks and mortar make a house but the laughter of children make a home. *Irish*
248. You cannot weigh worries but many a mother has a heavy heart. *Irish*
249. When children are little they make our heads ache; when grown, our hearts. *Italian*
250. Children are the poor man's treasure. *Japanese*
251. Excessive praise spoils the child. *Persian*
252. A mother's love will draw up from the depths of the sea. *Russian*
253. If the child does not cry the mother knows not its wants. *Russian*
254. By wise people, an appropriate observation is accepted even from a child. On the invisibility of the sun, is not the light of a lamp availed of? *Sanskrit*
255. They were scant o' bairns that brought you up. *Scottish*
256. Bairns are certain care but no sure joy. *Scottish*
257. Bachelor's wives and old maids' bairns are always well bred. *Scottish*
258. Ye'll learn your father to get bairns. *Scottish*
259. The bairn speaks in the fields what he heard by the hearth. *Scottish*
260. The mother who spoils her child fattens a serpent. *Spanish*
261. A child's love is water in a basket. *Spanish*

262. Children act in the village as they have learned at home.
     Swedish
263. If you want to learn something, listen to the children.   *Turkish*
264. He who has no children has one sorrow, he who has children
     has a thousand sorrows.   *Turkish*
265. If you have good children, why do you need wealth? And if you
     have bad children, again why do you need wealth?   *Turkish*
266. The father presented a vineyard to his son, but the son did not
     give his father a bunch of grapes.   *Turkish*
267. A disobedient child must eat the bread of sorrow.   *West Africa*
268. You complain about your neighbor's children. How about your
     own?   *West Africa*
269. Woe to the man who relies upon his children's help.   *Yugoslav*

Common Sense

270. Do not dress in leaf-made clothes when going to put out a
     fire.   *Chinese*
271. If there is no oil in the lamp, the wick is wasted.   *Chinese*
272. The fox invited the chicken to dinner; the chicken politely
     declined.   *Greek*
273. If you put it in the tank do not seek it in the well.   *India*.
274. If common sense rules from your head to your feet, you'll not
     wear a dunce cap or walk a wrong road.   *Irish*
275. Before you buy shoes, measure your feet.   *West Africa*
276. There are forty kinds of lunacy, but only one kind of common
     sense.   *West Africa*

Companions

277. Live with him who prays and you will pray; live with him who
     sings and you will sing.   *Arab*
278. The crow does not roost with the phoenix.   *Chinese*

279. Touch black paint and you will have black fingers. *Chinese*
280. Birds of a feather flock together. *English*
281. A man among children will be long a child; a child among men will soon be a man. *English*
282. A tree is known by its fruit. *English*
283. If you have no arrows in your quiver, do not go with archers. *German*
284. A dove has no place amongst the crows. *Greek*
285. Whatever is in the pot will come onto the ladle. *Hindustan*
286. In the friendship of an ass expect nothing but kicks. *India*
287. He who lives with the wolf learns to howl. *Italian*
288. The friend of the priest loses his religion; the friend of the doctor loses his health; the friend of the lawyer loses his substance. *Italian*
289. Know a horse by riding him; a person by associating with him. *Japanese*
290. A thief knows a thief and a saint a saint. *Persian*
291. Keep good company and ye will be counted one of them. *Scottish*
292. Eagles fly alone but sheep flock together. *Scottish*
293. Put two pennies in a purse and they'll creep together. *Scottish*
294. Leopards and goats do not associate with each other in herds. *West Africa*
295. If it is difficult to know a man, find out with whom he associates. You will then know him. *Yugoslav*

Competence

296. A good archer is known not by his arrows but by his aim. *English*
297. The good seaman can be recognized when the storm comes. *Greek*
298. The load of an elephant can be carried only by the elephant. *Hindustan*

299. Under a powerful general there are no feeble soldiers.
      Japanese
300. To a good rider, right or left makes no difference.   *Turkish*

Confidence

301. Confidence brings more to conversation than does wit.
      French
302. The man who has mounted an elephant will not fear the bark of
      a dog.   *India*
303. The biggest of serpents has no terrors for the eagle.   *Japanese*
304. What fear has he whose account is clean?   *Persian*

Conscience

305. The man whose conscience is easy will never fear a knock on the
      door at midnight.   *Chinese*
306. Better a good conscience without wisdom than wisdom without
      a good conscience.   *German*
307. A good conscience makes a soft pillow.   *German*
308. A good conscience makes a joyful countenance.   *German*
309. Conscience chastises the soul.   *Greek*
310. May we always have a clean shirt, a clean conscience and a bob
      in the pocket.   *Irish*
311. You don't have to live with the man you cheat, but you have to
      live with your conscience.   *Irish*
312. A good conscience is God's eye.   *Russian*
313. A safe conscience makes a sound sleep.   *Scottish*

Consequences

314. If you strike mud against the wall, even though it does not
      stick, it will leave a mark.   *Arab*

315. If you travel by boat, prepare for a wetting. *Chinese*
316. He shall reap hemp who sows hemp, and beans who sows beans. *Chinese*
317. Look not at thieves eating fish, rather look at them being punished. *Chinese*
318. When the upper beam is crooked, the lower must be awry. *Chinese*
319. He that blows in the fire must expect sparks in his eyes. *German*
320. From a wormy walnut tree you will gather wormy walnuts. *Greek*
321. If you play around the beehive you must expect to be stung. *Greek*
322. If you sleep with a dog you will rise full of fleas. *Greek*
323. Whoever jumps over the fence will sometimes tear his breeches. *Greek*
324. The butterfly that sports around the lamplight will surely burn her wings. *Greek*
325. If you plant a mango then you may eat a mango. *Hindustan*
326. He that digs a pit for another may fall into it himself. *Hindustan*
327. I sowed seeds of acacia; whence shall I eat raisins? *Hindustan*
328. If you bite a stone, your own teeth will be broken. *India*
329. One must accept the cow's kick as well as her milk and butter. *India*
330. The more you step on the dunghill, the more dirt you'll get into. *Irish*
331. He who is an ass and takes himself to be a stag finds his mistake when he comes to leap the ditch. *Italian*
332. Flies will never leave the shop of a sweetmaker. *Persian*
333. Where you saw wood, there the sawdust will fall. *Russian*
334. He must stoop who has a low door. *Scottish*
335. Let him cool in the skin he het in. *Scottish*
336. He who peeps through a hole may see what will vex him. *Spanish*
337. "If" and "when" were planted, and "nothing" grew. *Turkish*

338. It rained on the mountaintop, but it was the valley below that got flooded. *West Africa*
339. If you bring a firebrand into your hut then do not complain of the smoke. *West Africa*

Contentment

340. Go along with old shoes until God brings you new shoes. *Arab*
341. I have plenty of apples and pears, but my heart yearns for quince. *Armenian*
342. Be content with whatever you have. *Chinese*
343. With coarse food to eat, water to drink and the bended arm as a pillow, happiness may still exist. *Chinese*
344. No news is good news. *English*
345. A bird in the hand is worth two in the bush. *English*
346. He who has everything is content with nothing. *French*
347. If there are no thrushes, then one eats blackbirds. *French*
348. Contentment is worth more than riches. *German*
349. The mosque has fallen, but the pulpit stands. *Hindustan*
350. When the bed breaks, there is the ground to lie on. *India*
351. A harvest of peace is produced from a seed of content-ment. *India*
352. Stretch your limbs according to your sheet. *India*
353. Firelight will not let you read fine stories, but it's warm and you won't see the dust on the floor. *Irish*
354. A trout in the pot is worth two salmon in the sea. *Irish*
355. Be happy with what you have, and you will have plenty to be happy about. *Irish*
356. He who knows not when he has enough, is poor. *Japanese*
357. The sky is the same color wherever you go. *Persian*
358. If there is no apple one eats a little carrot. *Russian*
359. As long as the sun shines one does not ask for the moon. *Russian*

360. Desire upon desire cause the greatest sorrow; contentment, the greatest happiness. *Sanskrit*
361. Better a wee fire to warm you than a big fire to burn you. *Scottish*
362. Better to be the head of the commons than the tail of the gentry. *Scottish*
363. On a day when you can dine on dry bread in your own house, do not seek to eat tender peacocks in the house of another. *Spanish*
364. That which one cannot have one should not desire. *Swedish*
365. He who is contented has enough. *Swedish*
366. A thing that is out of my reach is useless to me. *West Africa*
367. A cow must graze where it is tied. *West Africa*
368. What is impossible to change is best to forget. *Yugoslav*
369. As we cannot do as we will, we will do as we can. *Yugoslav*

Cooperation

370. One cannot help many, but many can help one. *Chinese*
371. No matter how stout, one beam cannot support a house. *Chinese*
372. Two heads are better than one. *English*
373. If several join in an enterprise, then there is no disgrace should they fail. *Hindustan*
374. Three helping one another will do as much as six men singly. *Spanish*
375. In the forest, tree leans on tree, in a nation, man on man. *Yugoslav*

D

The clock strikes
differently every
hour.
Hindustani

Death
Desperation
Destiny
Differences
Drink

Death

376. Death sends his challenge in a gray hair. *Arab*
377. When you are dead, your sister's tears will dry as time goes on, your widow's tears will cease in another's arms, but your mother will mourn you until she dies. *Arab*
378. The first breath is the beginning of death. *English*
379. One had as well be nibbled to death by ducks as pecked to death by hens. *English*
380. Dead men tell no tales. *English*
381. When doctors differ, patients die. *English*
382. We should weep for men at their birth, and not at their death. *French*
383. Death is far better than the fear of death. *French*
384. Most men die of their medicines and not of their maladies. *French*
385. Gray hairs are death's blossoms. *German*
386. One has only to die to be praised. *German*
387. For death there is no medicine. *German*
388. Luck is for the few, death for the many. *German*
389. You cannot go to heaven unless you yourself die. *India.*
390. That which blossoms must also decay. *India*
391. Ink stains may be removed by washing, but natural dispositions disappear only in dying. *India.*
392. May you never die until you see your own funeral. *Irish*
393. The keening is best if the corpse left money. *Irish*
394. May you be across Heaven's threshold before the old boy knows you're dead. *Irish*
395. Better a coward than a corpse. *Irish*
396. There'll be many a dry eye at his death. *Irish*
397. Day by day death approaches, like the slaughter of a victim being led along step by step. *Sanskrit*

398. Wealth stops at the house, friends and relatives at the grave, but good deeds and evil deeds follow the dying man. *Sanskrit*
399. He that sits with his back to a draft, sits with his face to a coffin. *Spanish*
400. Death fears no man. *West Africa*
401. The dead are not seen in the company of the living. *West Africa*

Desperation

402. A drowning man takes hold of his own hair. *Greek*
403. Desperation is the mistress of the impossible. *Spanish*
404. He who falls into the sea will cling even to a snake. *Turkish*
405. Care avails nothing against fate. *Arab*

Destiny

406. Destiny has four feet, eight hands and sixteen eyes: How then shall the ill-doer with only two of each hope to escape? *Chinese*
407. If a man's fate is to have only eight-tenths of a pint of rice, though he traverse the country over, he cannot get a full pint. *Chinese*
408. He that was born under a three half-penny planet shall never be worth two pence. *English*
409. What must be, must be. *French*
410. If a man is his own ruin let him not blame fate. *Irish*
411. Nothing can be erased from God's book. *Irish*
412. He that is born of a hen must scratch. *Italian*
413. When its time has arrived, the prey comes to the hunter. *Persian*
414. He who is destined for the gallows will not be drowned. *Russian*
415. An unguarded object remains safe if protected by destiny; stricken by destiny, it perishes though well-guarded. *Sanskrit*

416. After happiness, sorrow; after sorrow, happiness; happiness and sorrow revolve like a disc. *Sanskrit*
417. A man may woo where he may, but he must marry where his fate is. *Scottish*
418. When God ordains that one should die in the dark, it avails nothing that one's father is a wax chandler. *Spanish*
419. One can choose the clover yet end up in weeds. *Swedish*
420. Blood that is to flow will not stay in the veins. *Turkish*
421. Let no man think he can escape his fate. *West Africa*

Differences

422. Variety is the spice of life. *English*
423. Whatever is natural possesses variety. *French*
424. Every tale can be told in a different way. *Greek*
425. The clock strikes differently every hour. *Hindustan*
426. The gait, speech, action and turban of every man differs from all others. *Hindustan*
427. A man with a nose is infamous among a hundred noseless men. *Hindustan*
428. There are as many characters as there are individuals. *India*
429. Ten men, ten minds. *Japanese*
430. If every day was a sunny day, who would not wish for rain? *Japanese*
431. John has one custom and Jack another. *Russian*
432. No two things are exactly alike. *West Africa*
433. Even the fingers on one's hand are not alike. *Yugoslav*

Drink

434. The drunken man laughs without cause. *Arab*
435. Whoever drinks on credit gets drunk more quickly. *Armenian*
436. To stop drinking, study a drunkard when you are sober. *Chinese*

437. Drink wine and have the gout; drink none and have it anyway. *English*

438. He that killeth when he is drunk is hanged when he is sober. *English*

439. Choose thy company before thy drink. *English*

440. A drunkard who has taken the pledge should never be locked up in a wine cellar. *French*

441. When your wine flask is full, many friends can be made. *Greek*

442. Do not trust in wine. *Greek*

443. If you drink even milk under a date tree, they will say it is toddy. *India*

444. Do not be talkative in an ale house. *Irish*

445. He'd go to mass every morning if holy water were whiskey. *Irish*

446. Before you call for one for the road, be sure you know the road. *Irish*

447. You take your health once too often to the whiskey shop until it gets broken. *Irish*

448. When you look at the world through the bottom of a glass, may you see someone ready to buy. *Irish*

449. Take physic for healing, soup for nourishment and sake for happy living. *Japanese*

450. The drunkard knows not the shame of wine nor the abstinent its glow. *Japanese*

451. Though the drunkard be in church, people will always suppose him to be in the public house. *Russian*

452. More are drowned in drink than in water. *Scottish*

453. It's a dry tale that doesn't end in a drink. *Scottish*

454. He speaks in his drink what he thinks in his drouth. *Scottish*

455. Wine has two defects: If you add water to it, you ruin it; if you do not add water, it ruins you. *Spanish*

456. He who drinks wine on credit gets twice drunk. *Turkish*

457. When the rich man falls down it is an accident; when a poor man falls, he is called drunk. *Turkish*

458. If you do not live near a wine palm you will not be tempted to drink palm wine. *West Africa*

459. If I cannot propose a toast, at least I can drink the wine. *Yugoslav*
460. It is the fool who fights the bottle and the wise man who drinks the wine. *Yugoslav*
461. Wine from a pot is better than water from a well. *Yugoslav*
462. The drunkard reforms when he keels into his grave. *Yugoslav*
463. Many more drown in the cup than sink at sea. *Yugoslav*

E

It is always necessary
to start from a truth
in order to teach an
error.

French

Envy
Equality
Error
Excuses
Experience

Envy

464. Compete, don't envy. *Arab*
465. Envy accomplishes nothing. *Greek*
466. It is not good for the eyes to smart in looking at another's goods. *India*
467. Lepers are always envious of those with simple sores. *Japanese*
468. When everyone praised the peacock for his beautiful tail, the birds cried out with one consent, "But look at his legs, and what a voice!" *Japanese*
469. It's the tortoise that discounts the value of a pair of fast legs. *Japanese*
470. In the hands of our neighbor, the morsel always appears big. *Russian*
471. The fishes envy the carp on account of his shears. *West Africa*
472. If envy would burn, there would be no use of wood. *Yugoslav*

Equality

473. He who rides the chair is a man like those who carry it. *Chinese*
474. What's sauce for the goose is sauce for the gander. *English*
475. The peasant reaches heaven as soon as the nobleman. *German*
476. Those who live in houses are proud, but there is a God even for those who live in huts. *India*
477. Six feet of earth makes us all of one size. *Italian*
478. He who sits in, and he who pulls the rickshaw, are alike men. *Japanese*
479. He who holds the stirrup is as good as he who mounts the horse. *Scottish*

Error

480. Rather a slip of the foot than a slip of the pen. *Arab*
481. What good is running if one is on the wrong road? *English*
482. A miss is as good as a mile. *English*
483. It is always necessary to start from a truth in order to teach an error. *French*
484. A wise man will not err twice in the same way. *Greek*
485. If you take the wrong hat from a meeting, make sure it doesn't belong to a big man. *Irish*
486. From seeing smoke rising from one house, we do not infer that there is a fire in another house. *Sanskrit*
487. He is always right who suspects that he is always making mistakes. *Spanish*
488. Through mistakes one becomes wise. *West Africa*
489. One mistake will never kill a man. *West Africa*
490. Every mistake has its own source. *West Africa*
491. First to make a mistake, first to be laughed at. *West Africa*

Excuses

492. They said to the camel bird (ostrich) "Carry!" It said, "I cannot, for I am a bird." They said "Then fly." It replied "I cannot, for I am a camel." *Arab*
493. Excuses are always mixed with lies. *Arab*
494. When they asked the fish "Have you news from the sea?" she answered, "I have much to say but my mouth is full of water." *Armenian*
495. Ask a kite for a feather and she will say she has just enough to fly." *English*
496. He who makes excuses accuses himself. *French*
497. To make excuses before they are needed is to blame one's self. *Spanish*

Experience

498. Ask the experienced rather than the learned. *Arab*
499. The tongue of experience has the most truth. *Arab*
500. To know the road ahead, ask those coming back. *Chinese*
501. Experience is a hard school but a fool will learn in no other. *Irish*
502. An old broom knows the dirty corners best. *Irish*
503. Sense bought by experience is better than two senses learned. *Irish*
504. Pinch yourself and know how others feel. *Japanese*
505. It is not the same to talk of bulls as to be in the bull ring. *Spanish*

F

A word
is not a
bird; once
flown you
can never
catch it.
Russian

Faults and Virtues
Finality
Fools
Foolishness
Friends and Enemies
Futile Expectations

Faults and Virtues

506. The first half of the night, think of your own faults, the second half, the faults of others. *Chinese*
507. He who tells me of my faults instructs me, he who tells me of my virtues robs me. *Chinese*
508. He never lies but when the holly's green. *English*
509. A fault denied is twice committed. *French*
510. If we had no faults we should take less pleasure in remarking those of others. *French*
511. Justifying a fault doubles it. *French*
512. The first and second faults may be forgiven, but the third stamps the miscreant. *Hindustan*
513. He sees the speck in another's eye, but not the film on his own. *Hindustan*
514. When faults are scrutinized, relationships cease. *India*
515. Wink at small faults, for you have great ones yourself. *Scottish*
516. It is well that all our faults are not written in our face. *Scottish*
517. You're a good seeker but an ill finder. *Scottish*

Finality

518. Four things cannot be brought back: a word spoken, an arrow discharged, the Divine decree, and past time. *Arab*
519. The swiftest horse cannot overtake the word once spoken. *Chinese*
520. Water and words are easy to pour, but impossible to recover. *Chinese*
521. All's well that end's well. *English*

522. He laughs best who laughs last. *English*
523. Everything passes, everything perishes, everything palls. *French*
524. It is too late to cover the well when the child is drowned. *German*
525. After conception, there is nothing for it but to bring forth. *India*
526. Spilt water cannot be gathered up again. *Japanese*
527. Once fallen, the blossom does not return to the branch. *Japanese*
528. The arrow which leaves the bow cannot come back. *Persian*
529. A word is not a bird; once flown you can never catch it. *Russian*
530. As the journey is ended by walking, so the debt is paid by paying. *Turkish*
531. Opportunities you have missed will not return. *West Africa*
532. No chicken will fall into the fire a second time. *West Africa*
533. Hours once lost cannot be regained. *Yugoslav*

Fools

534. The wise man tarries not to instruct the fool. *Chinese*
535. The fool in a hurry drinks his tea with a fork. *Chinese*
536. Whom Heaven hath endowed as a fool at his birth, it is a waste of instruction to teach. *Chinese*
537. A vacant mind is open to all suggestions, as a hollow building echoes all sounds. *Chinese*
538. A fool never admires himself so much as when he has committed a folly. *Chinese*
539. Expectation is the fool's income. *English*
540. It shows a great lack of intelligence to find answers to questions which are unanswerable. *French*
541. The young talk about what they are doing; the old about what they have done; fools about what they plan to do. *French*

542. He is a fool who drives the cow of a stranger's out of a field which is also a stranger's. *Hindustan*

543. A hundred wise men have the same opinion, but fools have every one their own. *India*

544. More know Tom-the-Fool than Tom-the-Fool knows. *Irish*

545. Ye didn't turn up when sense was being distributed. *Irish*

546. There's a fool born every minute and every one of them lives. *Irish*

547. Ye wouldn't do that if you had any flax on your distaff. *Irish*

548. When fools make mistakes, they lay the blame on Providence. *Irish*

549. He who knows but little presently outs with it. *Italian*

550. Learning without wisdom is a load of books on an ass's back. *Japanese*

551. If they sent you even to the sea, you would not be able to find water. *Persian*

552. The drum is boisterous to no avail; there is nothing in it. *Persian*

553. Silence is the answer to the fool. *Persian*

554. By the time I make a man of thee, I will myself have become a fool. *Persian*

555. If all fools wore white caps we should look like a flock of sheep. *Russian*

556. It is better to wander in a mountain pass with wild beasts than to live in the palace of the gods with a fool. *Sanskrit*

557. God send ye more sense and me more silver. *Scottish*

558. The first step in the ladder of folly is to believe oneself wise. *Spanish*

559. A wise man knows his own ignorance; a fool thinks he knows everything. *Spanish*

560. Wit without discretion is a sword in the hand of a fool. *Spanish*

561. It is easier for a camel to jump over a pit than for the stupid to grasp what you say. *Turkish*

562. By the time the fool has learned the game, the players have dispersed. *West Africa*

Foolishness

563. Do not order the tree to be cut down which gives you shade.   *Arab*

564. He fled from the rain and then sat down under the water-spout.   *Arab*

565. The ass went seeking horns and lost his ears.   *Arab*

566. He is looking for the donkey while sitting on it.   *Armenian*

567. He can't even pull on his own britches, and he's running off to Baghdad.   *Armenian*

568. Do not tear down the east wall to repair the west.   *Chinese*

569. To sing to the deaf, to talk with the dumb, and to dance for the blind are three foolish things.   *Hindustan*

570. Do not pull down the mosque in order to get one brick.   *Hindustan*

571. The child is in his arms, yet he proclaims it lost in the city.   *Hindustan*

572. It is foolish to hold a candle before the sun or turn a somersault before a monkey.   *India*

573. He wears bracelets on his wrists while his stomach is burning with hunger.   *India*

574. Is it necessary to dye a raven black?   *India*

575. Talking with a fool is like pouring water into an inverted pitcher.   *India*

576. Do not dig a mountain to rescue a mouse.   *India*.

577. Never send a chicken to bring home a fox.   *Irish*

578. He got up from the ground and sat on the ashes.   *Persian*

579. He puts his cheese in a bottle and rubs his bread on the outside.   *Persian*

580. The camel has gone into the minaret and cries, "I am hidden here, do not expose me."   *Persian*

581. Do not cover your neighbor's roof while your own is leaking.   *Russian*

582. He had fine knowledge of horse flesh who bought a goose to ride on.   *Scottish*

583. You're feared to be hanged for hurting your neck.   *Scottish*

584. The height of nonsense is suppin' sour milk with a fork. *Scottish*
585. If folly were grief, there would be weeping in every house. *Spanish*
586. Don't cross the stream to find water. *Swedish*
587. One does not chase that which is already caught. *Swedish*
588. He paid more for the lining than for the cloth. *Turkish*
589. A foolish act done over again will not improve things. *West Africa*
590. Why tell animals living in the water to drink? *West Africa*
591. You see the hut, yet you ask, "Where shall I go for shelter?" *West Africa*

Friends and Enemies

592. Let us quarrel with our friend rather than be too long friendly with our enemy. *Arab*
593. Have patience with a friend rather than lose him forever. *Arab*
594. An intelligent enemy is preferable to an ignorant friend. *Arab*
595. Predestined enemies will always meet in a narrow alleyway. *Chinese*
596. You can hardly make a friend in a year, but you can easily offend one in an hour. *Chinese*
597. If you have money and wine, your friends will be many. *Chinese*
598. A friend in need is a friend indeed. *English*
599. The church is full of his acquaintances; the pulpit would hold his friends. *English*
600. A hedge between keeps friendship green. *English*
601. When you turn the soup kettle upside down, your friends leave you. *French*
602. It is more shameful to distrust one's friends than to be deceived by them. *French*
603. Where there is no enemy it is safe fighting. *German*

604. Friendship is a plant we must often water. *German*
605. Everyone's companion is no one's friend. *German*
606. A life without a friend is a life without a sun. *German*
607. We can live without a brother, but not without a friend. *German*
608. To lose a friend, make him a loan. *Greek*
609. Friendship is not a fruit for enjoyment only, but also an opportunity for service. *Greek*
610. Not your friend but your enemy will tell you who you are. *Greek*
611. A good man finds all the world friendly. *Hindustan*
612. Though your enemy be a hundred miles off, act as if he were visible beside your bed. *India*
613. Prove a friend before you seek him. *Irish*
614. Men of the same trade are enemies. *Persian*
615. A friend turned enemy is the worst kind. *Russian*
616. Make friendship with the wolf, but keep your axe ready. *Russian*
617. A thousand friends are few; one enemy is too many. *Russian*
618. An untried friend is like an uncracked nut. *Russian*
619. A new friend is like a frozen stream in spring. *Russian*
620. He is wise that can make a friend of a foe. *Scottish*
621. If thy enemy is an ant, regard him as an elephant. *Turkish*
622. Boast to a stranger, complain only to your friends. *Yugoslav*
623. Show me a friend who will weep with me; those who will laugh with me I can find myself. *Yugoslav*

Futile Expectations

624. You cannot fill your belly by painting pictures of bread. *Chinese*
625. Though the ant works its heart out, it can never make honey. *English*
626. The frog wanted to be an ox and swelled up until he burst. *Greek*

627. From a broken violin do not expect fine music.   *Greek*
628. The fox that waited for the chickens to fall off their perching place died of hunger.   *Greek*
629. Do not look for aromatic words from a foul mouth.   *Greek*
630. The crane, hoping to eat dried fish when the sea dried up, wasted away in expectancy.   *India*
631. No matter how high the little bird soars, it cannot become a kite.   *India*
632. The pearls on the other side of the river are as large as palmyra fruits.   *India*
633. She has neither nose . nor ears, yet desires nose and ear rings.   *India*
634. It's no use going to the goat's house to look for wool.   *Irish*
635. One cannot lap up the ocean with a shell.   *Japanese*
636. He who remains hopeful of his neighbor's help will have to go to bed dinnerless.   *Persian*
637. One cannot learn to swim in a field.   *Spanish*
638. The frog saw the horse being shod and presented his feet also.   *Turkish*
639. From lean meat do not expect fat broth.   *Turkish*
640. A fire will not be quenched by adding more fuel.   *West Africa*
641. One cannot possibly bake bread for the entire world.   *Yugoslav*

G

Rogues listen not
to discourses
on honesty.
India

Good and Evil
Greed
Guests

Good and Evil

642. Evil people know one another. *Arab*
643. The willing contemplation of evil is vice. *Arab*
644. The word "yes" brings trouble, the word "no" leads to no evil. *Arab*
645. A man cannot become perfect in a hundred years; but he may become corrupt in less than a day. *Chinese*
646. Man will no more be virtuous without exhortation than a bell will sound without being struck. *Chinese*
647. Rotten wood cannot be carved. *Chinese*
648. To talk goodness is not good—only to do it is. *Chinese*
649. The door to virtue is heavy and hard to push. *Chinese*
650. Every evil comes to us on wings and goes away limping. *French*
651. When one evil comes, a million follow it. *Greek*
652. Every man is the guardian of his own honor. *Hindustan*
653. Concealed enmity or wickedness comes to light at last. *Hindustan*
654. It's often the most wicked who know the nearest path to the shrine. *Japanese*
655. To overcome evil is worth three pieces of gold; to have none in the first place is worth five. *Japanese*
656. Let a man so act by day that he may lie happily on his mat by night. *Japanese*
657. A thread will tie an honest man better than a rope will tie a knave. *Scottish*
658. Evil is a hill, everyone gets on his own and speaks about someone else's. *West Africa*
659. Evil knows the sleeping place of evil. *West Africa*
660. Evil enters like a needle and spreads like an oak tree. *West Africa*

661. It is not easy to meet good, but it is easy to recognize it. *Yugoslav*
662. A culprit is afraid of his own shadow. *Yugoslav*

Greed

663. Greed lessens what is gathered. *Arab*
664. If the camel gets his nose in the tent, his body will soon follow. *Arab*
665. Cleanse thy heart from greed, and thy foot shall remain free of fetters. *Arab*
666. Give him an inch and he'll take a mile. *English*
667. He has a larger eye than a stomach. *Greek*
668. If he is allowed to touch your finger, he will speedily seize your wrist. *Hindustan*
669. The greedy man stores all but friendship. *Irish*
670. Avarice closes the eyes of even a sensible man. Is it not greed that brings birds and fishes into nets? *Persian*
671. He is in the water up to the neck and is clamoring for a drink. *Russian*
672. Greedy folk have long arms. *Scottish*
673. One who grabs too much may lose it all. *Swedish*
674. Who asks at once for much returns home with an empty bag. *Yugoslav*

Guests

675. The guest of the hospitable learns hospitality. *Arab*
676. Only the innkeeper is unworried by his guests' big appetites. *Chinese*
677. Better to slight a guest than starve him. *Chinese*
678. To issue an invitation is to render ourselves responsible for our guest's happiness as long as he is under our roof. *French*

679. The guest is dearest when he is leaving. *German*
680. The other man's bread tastes sweeter. *Greek*
681. A person is a guest for one or two days, but becomes an intruder on the third. *Hindustan*
682. A guest between two houses will starve. *India*
683. Do not visit too often or too long. *Irish*
684. Constant company wears out its welcome. *Irish*
685. While there's fire in one's cooking stove, guests will never cease to arrive. *Japanese*
686. An uninvited guest is worse than a Tartar. *Russian*
687. Whether a child, or an old man, or a youth come to thy house, he is to be treated with respect, for of all men thy guest is thy superior. *Sanskrit*
688. Come uncalled, sit unserved. *Scottish*
689. A guest who breaks the dishes of his host is not soon forgotten. *West Africa*
690. When you set a meal before your guest, do not watch him eat. *West Africa*
691. The hunter who killed the game invites the guests. *West Africa*
692. An impatient guest seldom eats the fattest fowl. *West Africa*
693. A guest should not be unmindful of what he owes his host. *West Africa*
694. The place of an uninvited guest is behind the door. *Yugoslav*

H

The
best food
is that
which fills
the belly.
Arab

Habit
Health
Hindsight
Hunger

Habit

695. I dreamed a thousand new paths . . . I woke and walked my old one. *Chinese*
696. Filth is got rid of by washing; habit is not so easy to erase. *Hindustan*
697. Old habits are iron shirts. *Yugoslav*

Health

698. After dinner, rest. After supper, walk. *Arab*
699. No man is a good physician who has never been sick. *Arab*
700. One day in perfect health is much. *Arab*
701. Get the coffin ready and watch the man mend. *Chinese*
702. He that takes medicine and neglects diet wastes the skill of the physician. *Chinese*
703. When you shut out the sun from the window, the doctor comes in at the door. *Chinese*
704. An apple a day keeps the doctor away. *English*
705. The purse of the patient protracts his cure. *German*
706. Death is the doctor of all incurable ills. *Greek*
707. A disease comes with the speed of an elephant, and goes with the speed of an ant. *India*
708. A good laugh and a long sleep are the best cures in the doctor's book. *Irish*
709. Sickness is the physician's feast. *Irish*
710. The herb that can't be got is the one that brings relief. *Irish*
711. The more you think of dying, the better you will live. *Italian*
712. Who eats of but one dish never needs a physician. *Italian*
713. He who is afflicted can best appreciate health. *Persian*

714. See the pale color of my face and do not ask after my health.
      Persian

715. Expensive remedies are always useful, if not to the sick, to the
      chemist. *Russian*

716. He is a fool who makes his physician his heir. *Russian*

717. A patient will never recover his health merely from the descrip-
      tion of a medicine. *Sanskrit*

718. None are so well as they that hope to be better. *Scottish*

719. "Near dead" never filled the kirkyard. *Scottish*

720. When he sees death, then he is willing to accept fever.
      Turkish

721. Good thoughts are half of health. *Yugoslav*

Hindsight

722. When the ship has sunk, everyone knows how she could have
      been saved. *Italian*

723. Now that I put my hand to my head, I see there is no hat.
      Persian

Hunger

724. Grinding one's teeth does not fill one's belly. *Arab*

725. The best food is that which fills the belly. *Arab*

726. She was so hungry she couldn't stay for the parson to say
      grace. *English*

727. The way to a man's heart is through his stomach. *English*

728. Hunger is the best cook. *German*

729. Hunger is content with any food and sleep with any bed.
      Hindustan

730. If you ask the hungry man how many are two and two, he
      replies four loaves. *Hindustan*

731. Of what use is a blush on the face if the stomach is empty?
      India

732. No one ever washes himself so as never to require it again, nor does anyone ever eat so as to never hunger again. *India*
733. God never sent hunger without something to satisfy it. *Irish*
734. Happiness rarely keeps company with an empty stomach. *Japanese*
735. Even Fuji is without beauty to one who is hungry and cold. *Japanese*
736. Hunger is a good kitchen to a cold potato. *Scottish*
737. To a good appetite there is no bad bread. *Spanish*
738. There is no sauce like a good appetite. *Spanish*
739. A hungry monkey will not dance. *Turkish*
740. What do the satiated know of how the hungry feel? *Turkish*
741. No bread is too sharp to be refused by hunger. *Yugoslav*
742. To die of hunger is worse than to burn to death. *Yugoslav*

I

Making the beginning is one-third of the work.

Irish

Impossibilities
Industry and Sloth
Ingratitude

Impossibilities

743. Though the emperor be rich, he cannot buy one extra year. *Chinese*

744. No needle is sharp at both ends. *Chinese*

745. You cannot clap with one hand only. *Chinese*

746. There is no elbow that bends outward. *Chinese*

747. You can't make a silk purse out of a sow's ear. *English*

748. It's a bad bridge that is shorter than its stream. *German*

749. You cannot hide behind your finger. *Greek*

750. There is not room for two feet in one shoe. *Greek*

751. How can a sleeping man wake another who is asleep? *Hindustan*

752. Money seen in a dream will not be available for one's expenses. *India*

753. You cannot get milk from a male buffalo, nor butter by churning water. *India*

754. The hare, in its attempt to lay eggs like the tortoise, strained its eyes out and died. *India*

755. Water will not divide if you strike it with a stick. *India*

756. You can't take more out of a bag than what's in it. *Irish*

757. A knife will not cut its own handle. *Persian*

758. Two watermelons cannot be held in one hand. *Persian*

759. You cannot have the skin twice from the same bull. *Russian*

760. You cannot sew buttons on your neighbor's mouth. *Russian*

761. You can't drive straight on a twisting lane. *Russian*

762. The tip of a finger cannot be touched by itself. *Sanskrit*

763. You can't ring the bell and at the same time walk in the procession. *Spanish*

764. A mouth does not get sweet by talking about honey. *Turkish*

765. You cannot dig a well with a needle. *Turkish*

766. Even the best cooking pot will not produce food. *West Africa*

767. You cannot wipe the spots off a piebald horse.   *Yugoslav*

Industry and Sloth

768. Ask God for as much as you like, but keep a spade in your hand.   *Armenian*
769. The busy hand does not beg.   *Armenian*
770. Talk does not cook rice.   *Chinese*
771. Better return home and make a net than go down to the river and desire to get fishes.   *Chinese*
772. Work with the rising sun, rest with the setting sun.   *Chinese*
773. The devil finds work for idle hands.   *English*
774. All work and no play makes Jack a dull boy.   *English*
775. Rolling stones gather no moss.   *English*
776. To make an omelet, you have to break an egg.   *French*
777. God gives the nuts, but he does not crack them.   *German*
778. Not the butterfly but the bee produces the honey.   *Greek*
779. The plow that works is always shiny.   *Greek*
780. The gods sell us all things at the price of labor.   *Greek*
781. He who is too lazy to crack the nuts will have none to eat.   *Greek*
782. The thirsty person goes to the well, not the well to him.   *Hindustan*
783. Come, friend, and be doing something. It is better to work for nothing than to be idle.   *Hindustan*
784. The man who works like a slave may eat like a king.   *India*
785. A sleeping cat cannot catch a rat.   *India*
786. What you are planning to do tomorrow, do today; what you are going to do today, do right now.   *India*
787. There is no need to fear the wind if your haystacks are tied down.   *Irish*
788. Leisure is refined idleness.   *Irish*
789. Fat is not to be had without work.   *Irish*
790. Making the beginning is one-third of the work.   *Irish*

791. 'Tis the quiet people that do the work. *Italian*
792. In the house where the samisen is played all day long, there will be little rice in the larder. *Japanese*
793. "If" was married to "But" and they had a child named "Would-it-be." *Persian*
794. Better to beg than steal, but better to work than beg. *Russian*
795. No sweat, no sweet. *Scottish*
796. The fields are ever frozen for lazy pigs. *Swedish*
797. When you pray, pray with your hands upon the plow, then prayer power will bless your toil. *Swedish*
798. The bird on the wing finds something, the sitting bird nothing. *Swedish*
799. He who would climb a palm tree must not rest at its foot. *West Africa*
800. A man who does not leave his hut will bring nothing in. *West Africa*
801. He who would sweep the hut must not sit on the broom. *West Africa*
802. "I scratch the ground with both feet," says the hen. "If I do not find anything with one foot, I certainly shall with the other." *West Africa*
803. Better for the hands to be busy than the mouth. *West Africa*
804. Who wishes to rest when he gets old ought to work while he is young. *Yugoslav*

Ingratitude

805. He gets his passage for nothing and then winks at the captain's wife. *Arab*
806. Entertain the bedouin and he will steal your clothes. *Arab*
807. Warm up a frozen snake and she will bite you. *Armenian*
808. In the theater, free seats hiss first. *Chinese*
809. Don't look a gift horse in the mouth. *English*
810. Save a thief from the gallows and he will cut your throat. *English*

811. Who serves his country often serves an ingrate. *French*
812. Swift gratitude is the sweetest. *Greek*
813. To someone they offered an ass for a gift, and he looked at his teeth to ascertain his age. *Greek*
814. I gave him a staff for his support and he uses it to break my head. *India*
815. After eating the whole of the cucumber, he says the end of it is bitter. *India*
816. After the work is done, the carpenter is a rascal. *India*
817. The temple has fallen on the head of him that went to worship. *India*
818. If you beg on a foolscap, don't thank on a postcard. *Irish*
819. A satiated mouth soon forgets the benefactor. *Japanese*
820. Give the naked a piece of cloth and he will say it is too thick. *Russian*
821. Give a beggar a bed and he'll repay you with a louse. *Scottish*
822. He who has drunk his fill soon turns his back on the fountain. *Spanish*
823. To heap fresh kindnesses upon ungrateful men is the wisest but withal the most cruel revenge. *Spanish*
824. Scarcely has the hungry beggar-woman eaten her fill than she wants us to call her Madam. *Yugoslav*

J

He measures
others by
himself.

French

Judgment
Justice and Injustice

Judgment

825. Don't judge a book by its cover. *English*
826. He measures others by himself. *French*
827. Every man complains of his memory, but no man complains of his story. *French*
828. Do not judge until you have heard both sides of the argument. *Greek*
829. When a camel is at the foot of a mountain, then judge his height. *Hindustan*
830. He who would form a correct judgment of their tone must hear first one bell and then the other. *Italian*
831. He who judges others condemns himself. *Italian*
832. The fiddle is judged by its tune. *Russian*

Justice and Injustice

833. Though the sword of justice be sharp, it will not slay the innocent. *Chinese*
834. Of ten reasons a judge may have for deciding a case, nine will be unknown to the world. *Chinese*
835. Justice is ever on the side of the victor. *French*
836. The sword of justice has no scabbard. *French*
837. The poor man must suffer for the rich man's transgressions. *German*
838. The edge cuts and the sword has the credit; the soldiers fight and the general has the fame. *Hindustan*
839. If a man steals gold, he is put in prison. If he steals a land, he is made king. *Japanese*
840. To spare the ravening leopard is an act of injustice to the sheep. *Persian*

841. The bear does the dancing and the gypsy takes the money.
     Russian
842. The way of justice is mysterious. *Sanskrit*
843. They first hang a man, then try him. *Scottish*
844. Justice pleases few in their own homes. *Spanish*
845. The rich break the laws and the poor are punished for it.
     Spanish
846. The dog stole and the goat is being punished. *West Africa*
847. Injustice laughs by the table while justice weeps behind the
     door. *Yugoslav*

L

She will
love
tomorrow who
loved not
yesterday.
Italian

Laws
Love

Laws

848. Win your lawsuit and lose your money. *Chinese*
849. In making laws, severity; in administering laws, clemency. *Chinese*
850. It's an ill cause a lawyer thinks shame of. *English*
851. Men make laws, but women make morals. *French*
852. Liberty is the right to do whatever the laws permit. *French*
853. Useless laws diminish the authority of necessary ones. *French*
854. Go to law for a sheep and you lose your cow. *German*
855. As fast as laws are devised, their evasion is contrived. *German*
856. Lawsuits make the parties lean, the lawyers fat. *German*
857. When a law is made, the way to avoid it is discovered. *Italian*
858. A nobleman is always in the right when a peasant sues. *Russian*
859. The law is like the axle of a carriage; you can turn it wherever you please. *Russian*
860. A good lawyer may be an ill neighbor. *Scottish*
861. Laws, like the spider's web, catch the fly and let the hawk go free. *Spanish*
862. When a bribe enters the door, laws get out at the chimney. *Turkish*
863. More laws cause more confusion and more difficulties. *Yugoslav*
864. Where there is no law, there can be no infraction of the same. *Yugoslav*

Love

865. Faults are thick where love is thin. *English*
866. Love is blind. *English*

867. Love is not to be trifled with. *French*
868. There is one who kisses, and one who offers the other cheek. *French*
869. Who loves well, forgets slowly. *French*
870. The torch of love is lit in the kitchen. *French*
871. He who hates is to be pitied, but he who loves is to be pitied more. *German*
872. Love can turn the cottage into a golden palace. *German*
873. Love and a cough will not let themselves be hid. *German*
874. A lovelorn cook oversalts the porridge. *German*
875. The heart that loves is always young. *Greek*
876. The ways of love are peculiar to itself. *Hindustan*
877. Life is no longer one's own when the heart is fixed on another. *Hindustan*
878. When the heart clings to a lover, who cares what caste he be? *India*
879. If you live in my heart, you live rent-free. *Irish*
880. He who has love in his breast has ever the spurs at his flanks. *Italian*
881. He saith little that loveth much. *Italian*
882. He who is not impatient is not in love. *Italian*
883. Love feedeth only upon love. *Italian*
884. He understands little of love who is forever speaking of love to his lady. *Italian*
885. Love is a thing that sharpens all our wits. *Italian*
886. He who is lucky in love should never play cards. *Italian*
887. She will love tomorrow who loved not yesterday. *Italian*
888. Who travels for love, finds a thousand miles only one mile. *Japanese*
889. The lovelorn maiden under the plum tree forgets that the kettle is simmering on the hibachi. *Japanese*
890. Love does not recognize a difference between peasant and mikado. *Japanese*
891. Love and perfume cannot be hidden. *Persian*
892. Lovers write their pledges on the horns of deer. *Persian*
893. A lass that has many wooers often chooses the worst. *Scottish*

894. Love kills with golden arrows. *Spanish*
895. Love is a furnace, but it will not cook the stew. *Spanish*
896. He who finds not love finds nothing. *Spanish*
897. It is never too far to the home of your beloved. *Swedish*
898. Gift exchanges make love last longer. *Swedish*
899. Before you love, learn to run through snow leaving no footprints. *Turkish*
900. When two hearts are one, even the king cannot separate them. *Turkish*
901. A lovesick person looks in vain for a doctor. *West Africa*

M

He
that has
a bonny
wife needs
more than
two eyes.

Scottish

Marriage
Misfortune and Fortune
Money

Marriage

902. My husband is not jealous, though my lover came seeking me with a lighted candle in his hand.   *Arab*

903. Wedlock is like a place under siege; those within want to get out and those without want to get in.   *Arab*

904. The joys of life are porridge and soup, a donkey to ride and a wife to drive it.   *Arab*

905. More belongs to marriage than four bare legs in a bed.   *English*

906. Who marries for love without money has good nights and sorry days.   *English*

907. Marriage teaches you to live alone.   *French*

908. You are a wife's friend at the time of earning and bringing, but you are a mother's son when you are tired and wearied.   *India*

909. A priest will perform your marriage ceremony, but he will not manage your house.   *India*

910. What is the world to a man whose wife is a widow?   *Irish*

911. It's a lonely washing that hasn't a man's shirt in it.   *Irish*

912. Let the man that you marry have an old maid for a mother.   *Irish*

913. If the hen crows instead of the cock, there won't be peace in the fowlyard.   *Japanese*

914. If you go to war, pray; if you go on a sea journey, pray twice; but pray three times when you are going to be married.   *Russian*

915. Having a good wife and rich cabbage soup; other things seek not.   *Russian*

916. A man without a wife is like a man in winter without a fur cap.   *Russian*

917. Next to no wife at all, a good one is best.   *Scottish*

918. A dish of married love soon grows cold.   *Scottish*

919. Woe is the wife who lacks a tongue, but well's the man who gets her.   *Scottish*

920. Never seek a wife until ye ken what to do with her. *Scottish*
921. He that has a bonny wife needs more than two eyes. *Scottish*
922. Better half hanged than ill married. *Scottish*
923. Never marry a widow unless her first husband was hanged.
      Scottish
924. He who tells his wife all is but newly married. *Scottish*
925. Every man can guide an ill wife except him that has her. *Scottish*
926. All are good lasses, but where do the ill wives come from?
      Scottish
927. If your wife tells you to throw yourself off a cliff, pray to God
      that it is a low one. *Spanish*
928. Sad is the home where the hen crows and the cock is si-
      lent. *Spanish*
929. A good wife is the workmanship of a good husband. *Spanish*
930. Before you marry, think what you are doing. *Spanish*
931. If you look for a faultless woman, you will remain a bache-
      lor. *Turkish*
932. Once in forty years do what your wife says. *Turkish*
933. Buy all the presents you will, if a woman does not love you, she
      is bound to marry another. *West Africa*
934. Differences between husband and wife should not be aired in
      the marketplace. *West Africa*
935. Where there is no wife, there is no home. *Yugoslav*
936. It is sometimes well to obey a sensible wife. *Yugoslav*

Misfortune and Fortune

937. Fortune is with you for an hour, and against you for ten.
      Arab
938. After sorrow comes joy. *Arab*
939. If the wind blows at every crevice, it enters at every door.
      Arab
940. Throw him into the river and he will rise with a fish in his
      mouth. *Arab*

941. If I were to trade in winding sheets, no one would die.   *Arab*
942. Blessings never come in pairs and ills never come alone.   *Chinese*
943. While a man is driving a tiger from his front door, a wolf is entering the back.   *Chinese*
944. On the day your horse dies and your gold vanishes, your relatives are like strangers on the road.   *Chinese*
945. If I were to fall backwards, I would break my nose.   *English*
946. It never rains, but it pours.   *English*
947. If he flings a penny in the air, a dollar will come down to him.   *English*
948. Misfortunes never come singly.   *English*
949. We must learn from life how to suffer it.   *French*
950. He who has not tasted bitter, knows not what sweet is.   *German*
951. Fortune and misfortune are two buckets in a well.   *German*
952. One gets pearls without asking, and another cannot obtain alms even by begging.   *Hindustan*
953. There is no tree that the wind does not reach.   *Hindustan*
954. A coming misfortune must be borne with patience; when it is gone you are liberated.   *Hindustan*
955. All are ready to be partners in a man's successes, none in his misfortunes.   *India*
956. Tell your troubles to yourself and your happinesses to the world.   *India*
957. When the elephant sinks in a pit, even the frog gives him a backward kick.   *India*
958. Without being hammered, a stone cannot become a god.   *India*
959. If I bet on the tide, it wouldn't come in.   *Irish*
960. May as well whistle jigs to a milestone as tell troubles to you.   *Irish*
961. He who would have no trouble in this world must not be born in it.   *Italian*
962. A sorrow is an itching place that is made worse by scratching.   *Japanese*

963. The heaviest rains fall on the leakiest house. *Japanese*
964. Think about the misfortunes of others, that you may be satisfied with your own lot. *Japanese*
965. A man's own breast is the best wallet to carry his troubles in. *Japanese*
966. There's always a bee to sting a weeping face. *Japanese*
967. Adversity is the source of strength. *Japanese*
968. Keep misfortune for three years; it may turn out to be useful. *Japanese*
969. When fortune comes to a house, the devil accompanies it to the door. *Japanese*
970. Advise and counsel him. If he does not listen, let adversity teach him. *Japanese*
971. A potful of luck is better than a sackful of wisdom. *Russian*
972. Walk fast and you catch misfortune; walk slowly and it catches you. *Russian*
973. Fortune and misfortune dwell in the same courtyard. *Russian*
974. Good fortune wears a pretty dress but its underclothes do not bear investigation. *Russian*
975. Even in hell, the peasant will have to serve the landlord; for while the latter is boiling in a cauldron, the former will have to put wood under it. *Russian*
976. Running away through fear of a scorpion, he falls into the jaws of a poisonous snake. *Sanskrit*
977. One gets another boil on top of the previous one. *Sanskrit*
978. He that has his hand in the lion's mouth must take it out the best way he can. *Scottish*
979. Fancy was a bonny dog, but Fortune took the tail from it. *Scottish*
980. Trouble will rain on those who are already wet. *Spanish*
981. I wept when I was born, and every day explains why. *Spanish*
982. Compare your griefs with other men's and they will seem less. *Spanish*
983. I don't want the cheese; I just want to get out of the trap. *Spanish*
984. It won't get better until worse has passed. *Swedish*

985. He ran away from the rain and was caught in a hailstorm. *Turkish*
986. If you have escaped the jaws of the crocodile while bathing in the river, you will surely meet a leopard on the way. *West Africa*
987. Sorrow is like a precious treasure, shown only to friends. *West Africa*
988. In the midst of bad luck, man shows what he is made of. *Yugoslav*
989. Misfortune never declares a holiday. *Yugoslav*
990. Misfortune neither plows nor sows, nevertheless it thrives. *Yugoslav*
991. Some people can make lead float where others will see their straw sink. *Yugoslav*
992. By the side of luck stands misfortune. *Yugoslav*
993. If Fortune does not wait for you, you cannot overtake her even with the fastest steed. *Yugoslav*

Money

994. He that has no money has no friends. *Arab*
995. One coin in the empty money box makes more noise than when it is full. *Arab*
996. A girl with a golden cradle doesn't remain long in her father's house. *Armenian*
997. For sins you cry, but for debts you pay. *Armenian*
998. A poor man associating with a rich man will soon be too poor to buy even a pair of breeches. *Chinese*
999. He has a hole under his nose that all his money runs into. *English*
1000. A penny saved is a penny earned. *English*
1001. Money makes the mare go. *English*
1002. A fool and his money are soon parted. *English*
1003. All is not gold that glitters. *English*
1004. A purse without money is but a piece of leather. *English*

1005. A covetous man makes a halfpenny of a farthing, and a liberal man makes sixpence of it. *English*

1006. He who has money receives more. *French*

1007. The price spoils the pleasure. *French*

1008. His money certifies the judgments of his intelligence. *French*

1009. Lending money to a man causes him to lose his memory. *French*

1010. Good bargains empty our pockets. *German*

1011. Five drachmas in the hand is better than ten drachmas on paper. *Greek*

1012. When you know you are about to lose all your wealth, then you had better give half of it away. *Hindustan*

1013. Let the money go as long as credit remains. *Hindustan*

1014. The offense given by not lending is to be preferred to the annoyance endured after lending. *India*

1015. You cannot purchase wit with wealth. *India*

1016. A heavy purse makes a light heart. *Irish*

1017. Sweet is the voice of the man who has wealth. *Irish*

1018. Does your neighbor bore you? Lend him some money. *Italian*

1019. To him who has no money, all things are lacking. *Italian*

1020. He who finds no money in his own purse is still less likely to find it in that of others. *Italian*

1021. The best way to make gold is to have a good fortune and spend little of it. *Italian*

1022. He who wants Lent to seem short should contract a debt to be paid at Easter. *Italian*

1023. The money you refuse will never do you good. *Italian*

1024. One ducat in your purse does you more honor than ten that you have spent. *Italian*

1025. That crown is well spent which saves you ten. *Italian*

1026. Who would make money must begin by spending it. *Italian*

1027. He who pays well is master of everybody's purse. *Italian*

1028. If a few sen do not go, many sen will not come. *Japanese*

1029. Do not look at the gold pieces you won; rather consider those you might have lost. *Japanese*

1030. Credit is better than wealth. *Persian*

1031. I pay money and beat a drum under the Shah's nose. *Persian*

1032. Where gold speaketh, all is silent. *Russian*

1033. In the next world, usurers have to count red-hot coins with bare hands. *Russian*

1034. A penniless man goes fast through the market. *Scottish*

1035. He who would be rich has not to pick up money, but to diminish his wants. *Spanish*

1036. When two friends have a common purse, one sings and the other weeps. *Spanish*

1037. Receive your money before you give a receipt for it, and take a receipt before you pay for it. *Spanish*

1038. A man's wealth may be superior to the man. *West Africa*

1039. Love of money is the undoing of men. *West Africa*

1040. A castle offered for a dinar is dear when you have no dinar. *Yugoslav*

1041. The jingle of money oftentimes kills the voice of justice. *Yugoslav*

P

If everyone gives
a kopeck, the poor
will have a ruble.

Russian

Patience
Persistence
Poverty
Preferable Alternatives
Prematurity
Pride

Patience

1042. The remedy against bad times is to be patient with them. *Arab*
1043. When you are an anvil, be patient; when a hammer, strike. *Arab*
1044. Patience and a mulberry leaf will make a silk gown. *Chinese*
1045. Everything comes to him who waits. *English*
1046. Patience is bitter, but its fruit is sweet. *French*
1047. Patience is a plaster for all pain. *French*
1048. Patience is often better than medicine. *German*
1049. Patience is the door of joy. *German*
1050. Patience caught the nimble hare. *Greek*
1051. Patience cures many an old complaint. *Irish*
1052. He that hath no patience, hath nothing at all. *Italian*
1053. The string of a man's sack of patience is generally tied with a slip knot. *Japanese*
1054. The future belongs to him who knows how to wait. *Russian*
1055. There is summer and there is winter; what need for hurry? *Turkish*
1056. Patience can break through iron doors. *Yugoslav*

Persistence

1057. If you cannot take things by the head, then take them by the tail. *Arab*
1058. Great things can be reduced to small things, and small things can be reduced to nothing. *Chinese*
1059. Three feet of ice are not frozen in one day. *Chinese*
1060. A bar of iron, continually ground, becomes a needle. *Chinese*
1061. Little strokes fell great oaks. *English*
1062. Practice makes perfect. *English*

1063.   If at first you don't succeed, try, try, again.   *English*
1064.   A road of a thousand miles begins with the first step.   *English*
1065.   There is no mortar that time shall not loosen.   *French*
1066.   He that would climb the ladder must begin at the bottom.
        German
1067.   If you seek well, you will find.   *Greek*
1068.   He who has lost his way in the morning cannot be said to have
        gone astray if he finds the way at night.   *Hindustan*
1069.   He that searcheth shall find, though he seek in deep water.
        But what can the poor sinner obtain who sits inactive on the
        shore?   *Hindustan*
1070.   If you throw a handful of stones, one at least will hit.   *India*
1071.   If you remove stone after stone, even a mountain will be
        leveled.   *India*
1072.   Fall seven times, stand up the eighth time.   *Japanese*
1073.   If you wish to learn the highest truth, you must begin with the
        alphabet.   *Japanese*
1074.   An apprentice becomes an expert by and by.   *Persian*
1075.   Step by step, one should ascend the stairs.   *Persian*
1076.   Hair by hair, you may pluck out the whole beard.   *Russian*
1077.   If you would be Pope, you can think of nothing else.
        Spanish
1078.   When a shepherd has a mind to do so, he will get you milk
        from a he-goat.   *Turkish*
1079.   Many drops will fill the pot.   *West Africa*
1080.   The monkey learns to jump by trying again and again.   *West
        Africa*

Poverty

1081.   Riches disclose bad qualities which poverty conceals.   *Arab*
1082.   The rich man plans for tomorrow, the poor man for today.
        Chinese

1083.   Better die ten years early than live ten years poor.   *Chinese*
1084.   The rich add riches to riches; the poor add years to years.
         Chinese
1085.   The man who has does not understand the man who has not.
         Chinese
1086.   The poor pilgrim laughs at the highwayman.   *Japanese*
1087.   It is the poor who give alms to the poor.   *Japanese*
1088.   From poverty to profusion is a hard journey, but the way back
         is easy.   *Japanese*
1089.   When drinking sake, remember the poverty of your family.
         Japanese
1090.   Troubles rain from walls and doors for a poor man.   *Persian*
1091.   That which changes a lion's temperament into that of a fox is
         poverty, poverty, and poverty.   *Persian*
1092.   Poverty is the heritage of poverty.   *Russian*
1093.   Who has nothing owes nothing.   *Russian*
1094.   If everyone gives a kopeck, the poor will have a ruble.
         Russian
1095.   The desires of the poor spring up and perish.   *Sanskrit*
1096.   The defect of poverty is the destroyer of a host of virtues.
         Sanskrit
1097.   Poverty is a pain but not a disgrace.   *Scottish*
1098.   When your own possessions are gone, those of another are of
         little use.   *West Africa*

Preferable Alternatives

1099.   Better a diamond with a flaw than a pebble without one.
         English
1100.   Half a loaf is better than none.   *English*
1101.   Better late than never.   *English*
1102.   To be redheaded is better than to be without a head.   *Irish*
1103.   Better wisdom than riches.   *Swedish*

1104. Better coarse bread than none to eat. *Swedish*

Prematurity

1105. Do not count the days of a month which may never belong to you. *Arab*
1106. With one hand he feeds the hens, with the other he searches for eggs. *Armenian*
1107. Don't count your chickens before they're hatched. *English*
1108. Chickens are slow in coming from unlaid eggs. *German*
1109. Never promise a fish until it's caught. *Irish*
1110. Do not sell the skin before catching the gazelle. *Persian*
1111. He who anticipates good fortune risks it by his presumption. *Spanish*
1112. Don't turn up your trousers before you get to the brook. *Turkish*
1113. Don't go selling the hide as long as the bear remains in his hole. *Yugoslav*

Pride

1114. He that is proud of his fine clothes gets his reputation from his tailor. *English*
1115. When a proud man hears another praised, he thinks himself injured. *English*
1116. Pride leaves home on horseback, but returns on foot. *German*
1117. It is easier to lift the mountain on the point of a needle than to root out pride from the heart. *German*
1118. The barber washes everyone's feet, but thinks it beneath him to wash his own. *Hindustan*
1119. His prosperity is fled, but his pride remains. *Hindustan*
1120. He that exalteth himself shall be humbled. *Hindustan*

1121. The house of pride is usually empty. *India*
1122. The peacock, having danced in pride, becomes crestfallen on seeing its ugly legs. *India*
1123. Pride is the author of every sin. *Irish*
1124. Brag not of the honor of ancestors. All you have is your own. *Swedish*

Q

Wrath begins in
madness and ends in
repentance.

Arab

Quarrels

Quarrels

1125. Wrath begins in madness and ends in repentance. *Arab*

1126. If they had not dragged me from under him, I would have killed him. *Arab*

1127. Whilst wrangling over a quarter of pig, you lose a flock of sheep. *Chinese*

1128. When the heron and the oyster seize each other, the fisherman reaps the benefit. *Chinese*

1129. A man that will fight may find a cudgel in every hedge. *English*

1130. Quarrels would not last long if the wrongs were all on one side. *French*

1131. The snappish cur always has torn ears. *French*

1132. Not to be on speaking terms is better than quarreling. *India*

1133. When two quarrel, a third profits by it. *India*

1134. A minute's parlaying is better than a week's fighting. *Irish*

1135. Who seeks a quarrel will find it near at hand. *Italian*

1136. The dispute which has only one side is easily settled. *Italian*

1137. The second word makes the fray. *Japanese*

1138. Brothers quarrel like thieves inside a house, but outside their swords leap out in each other's defense. *Japanese*

1139. If two men quarrel, even their dogs will have a difference. *Japanese*

1140. When families quarrel, outsiders deride. *Japanese*

1141. A bad peace is better than a good quarrel. *Russian*

1142. It's an ill fight where he that wins has the worst of it. *Scottish*

1143. He who has a handsome wife, a castle on the frontier, or a vineyard on the highway, will never lack for quarrels. *Spanish*

1144. It is seldom the fault of one when two argue. *Swedish*

1145. If you say "all right," there will be no quarrel in the bath. *Turkish*

1146. Every tree has a thick end, and every quarrel has a cause. *West Africa*

1147. Better a spoon of juice in peace than a table laden with food in quarrel. *Yugoslav*

R

He who bears the burden on his shoulders knows the weight.

India

Rationalization
Reality
Relativity
Religion
Resignation

Rationalization

1148. Because the cat was given no meat, he said it was Friday. *Armenian*
1149. To the bad driver, the mules are always to blame. *Greek*
1150. He that cannot dance claims the floor is uneven. *Hindustan*
1151. He fell down and said he was bowing to a god; he got swollen and claimed he was getting fat. *India*
1152. The fox has no desire for cherries because he has not learned how to climb the tree. *Italian*
1153. He is alive for he cannot afford a funeral. *Persian*
1154. "Why fuss about it?" said the crane after the eel had slipped away. "I never liked fish anyway." *West Africa*

Reality

1155. It is only when the cold season comes that we know the pine and cypress to be evergreens. *Chinese*
1156. A whitewashed crow soon shows black again. *Chinese*
1157. If you walk on snow you cannot hide your footprints. *Chinese*
1158. There is no rose without a thorn. *English*
1159. A diamond is valuable though it lie on a dunghill. *English*
1160. Beard and mantle do not make one a philosopher. *German*
1161. He keeps Lent because he has nothing to eat. *Greek*
1162. The pig, even dressed in silks, is a pig. *Greek*
1163. There is no concealing pregnancy from the midwife. *Hindustan*
1164. No proof is required of what is before our eyes. *Hindustan*
1165. The humpback alone knows how he can lie comfortably. *India*

1166. He who bears the burden on his shoulders knows its weight. *India*
1167. Whatever is in the pot flows out at the spout. *India*
1168. You cannot add symmetry to a finished house. *India*
1169. Do not expect waterlilies in every pond. *India*
1170. Those who travel on horseback know nothing of the toil of those who travel on foot. *Japanese*
1171. When a whole hundred has come, surely we have got ninety. *Persian*
1172. The ass is the same ass even when his halter has been changed. *Persian*
1173. Every round thing is not a walnut. *Persian*
1174. He whose feet has the chilblains feels the pain. *Persian*
1175. The goldsmith knows the value of gold, and a gem seller appreciates gems. *Persian*
1176. He who sows barley cannot gather wheat. *Persian*
1177. Though you take Jesus' ass to Mecca, he will still be an ass when he returns. *Persian*
1178. By slitting the ears and cutting the tail, a dog is still a dog, not a horse, not an ass. *Sanskrit*
1179. A dog does not resent being called a dog. *West Africa*
1180. The child of a leopard is a leopard. *West Africa*

Relativity

1181. Where there are no green trees, the castor oil bush is regarded as one. *India*
1182. The frog who has never seen the sea thinks the well a fine stretch of water. *Japanese*
1183. To the ant, a few drops of rain is a flood. *Japanese*
1184. Where the camel is sold for a cent, the ass has no actual value. *Persian*
1185. He who has never seen a castle will admire a pigpen. *Yugoslav*

Religion

1186. You honor dead Buddhas, but the living Buddhas you do not honor. *Chinese*
1187. In good times we forget to burn incense; in hard times we embrace the Buddha's feet. *Chinese*
1188. They that are in hell think there is no heaven. *English*
1189. God helps those who help themselves. *English*
1190. If the triangles made a god, they would give him three sides. *French*
1191. Prayer is a cry of hope. *French*
1192. The devil laughs if a thief steals from another thief. *French*
1193. The universe is a thought from God. *German*
1194. Religion that is built wholly on theology alone can never be wholly moral. *German*
1195. A pack of cards is the devil's prayerbook. *German*
1196. The fewer the words, the better the prayer. *German*
1197. How wise of God to plan death at the end of life. *German*
1198. Why burn oil before the ikon while you swear at God? *Greek*
1199. The devil invented war and fools practice it. *Greek*
1200. Move yourself and God will assist you. *Greek*
1201. The devil met a wicked woman and he got frightened. *Greek*
1202. Light your lamp first at home and only afterwards at the mosque. *Hindustan*
1203. If I do well, it will be ascribed to Providence; if ill, to myself. *Hindustan*
1204. No one has seen God; we know his existence by reason. *Hindustan*
1205. God never closed one gap without opening another. *Irish*
1206. You worship God in your way and I'll worship Him in His. *Irish*
1207. He who leaves God out of his reckoning does not know how to count. *Italian*
1208. Begin your web and God will supply the thread. *Italian*

1209. One word of thanks reaches up to heaven. *Japanese*
1210. One good deed is better than three days of fasting at a shrine. *Japanese*
1211. The bell calls to church, but never goes there itself. *Russian*
1212. He who throws even a splinter to cover a widow's home will be protected by God. *Russian*
1213. Our souls are God's; our bodies belong to the Czar. *Russian*
1214. Go before God with justice, before the judge with money. *Russian*
1215. Where God builds his church, there the devil has his chapel. *Russian*
1216. Give the devil a candle as well; you never know whom you may please. *Russian*
1217. Even the thief prays to God, but the devil gets hold of his prayers. *Russian*
1218. God is always where we don't look for him. *Russian*
1219. Pray to God, but do not offend the devil either. *Russian*
1220. Pray to God but keep rowing to the shore. *Russian*
1221. With God go over the sea, without Him do not go over the threshold. *Russian*
1222. Non-injury is the highest religion. *Sanskrit*
1223. The closer to the church one lives, the more often he is late for mass. *Yugoslav*
1224. God shuts one door in order to open a hundred doors. *Yugoslav*

Resignation

1225. He who has put his head into the mortar should not be afraid of the bellows. *Hindustan*
1226. Since my house must be burned, I may as well warm myself at it. *Italian*
1227. When the water is overhead, what difference if it be one fathom or a hundred fathoms? *Persian*

S

The
drunkard
and the
fool
never
keep
secrets.
Greek

Secrecy
Sequences
Speech
Superfluity
Superiority
Suspicion

Secrecy

1228. Do not tell secrets in front of servants. *Arab*
1229. A man's folly ought to be his greatest secret. *English*
1230. Every betrayal of a secret is the fault of the person who confided it. *French*
1231. Secret charity and secret patience are best. *German*
1232. The drunkard and the fool never keep secrets. *Greek*
1233. If only one knows it, it is secret; if two know it, it is public. *India*
1234. He who comes to you with a secret to tell goes away with two. *Irish*
1235. He who wishes another to guard his secret should guard it himself first. *Italian*
1236. Never reveal the bottom of your purse or the bottom of your mind. *Italian*
1237. The bosoms of the wise are the tombs of secrets. *Japanese*
1238. Talk quietly; even the walls have ears. *Persian*
1239. When the scabbards are broken, we can no longer hide our swords. *Russian*
1240. Keep no secrets from your doctor, your confessor, and your lawyer. *Spanish*
1241. Secrecy is the soul of business. *Spanish*
1242. A discreet man will always be ignorant of more than he knows. *Spanish*

Sequences

1243. When the fingers fall to scratching, the thumb follows along. *Chinese*
1244. Where the needle goes, the thread follows. *India*
1245. Where the head goes, the feet will go also. *Turkish*
1246. I am scratching myself where I am itching. *Yugoslav*

Speech

1247. More than one war has been caused by a single word. *Arab*

1248. The sword wounds the body, but words wound the soul. *Arab*

1249. If you wish to know the mind of a man, listen to his speech. *Chinese*

1250. To lock up mischief, keep your mouth closed. *Chinese*

1251. Two good talkers are not worth one good listener. *Chinese*

1252. Words spoken may fly away, but the writing brush will leave its mark. *Chinese*

1253. Fair words make me look to my purse. *English*

1254. The tongue of a fool carves a piece of his heart to all that sit near him. *English*

1255. What orators lack in depth, they make up for in length. *French*

1256. We must have reasons for speech, but we need none for silence. *French*

1257. The less one thinks, the more one speaks. *French*

1258. Speak little and well if you would be esteemed as a man of merit. *French*

1259. The spoken word belongs half to him who speaks and half to him who hears. *French*

1260. The wise man weighs his words on the goldsmith's scale. *German*

1261. Words often do worse than blows. *German*

1262. A man has two ears and one mouth that he hear much and speak little. *German*

1263. Not speech, but facts, convince. *Greek*

1264. The sword in its scabbard, and the tongue in its place, will never cause tears to be shed. *Greek*

1265. No sooner have you spoken than what you have said becomes the property of another. *Hindustan*

1266. That which is in the mind comes into the mouth. *Hindustan*

1267. From opening the mouth, seven ills may ensue. *Hindustan*

1268. Where there is a surfeit of words, there is a famine of intelligence. *India*

1269. One lash to a good horse, one word to a sensible man. *India*
1270. Though we teach an ass by speaking in his ear, we obtain nothing but braying. *India*
1271. One that speaks little wins the day, one that speaks much bears the blows. *India*
1272. First weigh your words, then speak openly. *India*
1273. Soft words butter no turnips, but they won't harden the heart of the cabbage either. *Irish*
1274. A sweet tongue is seldom without a sting to its root. *Irish*
1275. God gave us two ears and one mouth and we should use them in the same proportion. *Irish*
1276. Ah, you've kissed the Blarney stone. *Irish*
1277. Don't let your tongue say what your head may pay for. *Italian*
1278. Many have suffered for talking; none ever suffered for keeping silent. *Italian*
1279. Worse than a mute is he who does not speak clearly. *Italian*
1280. What shall I say when it is better to say nothing? *Persian*
1281. To quarrel with a man of good speech is better than to converse with a man of rude address. *Sanskrit*
1282. Where frogs are the croakers, there silence is becoming. *Sanskrit*
1283. Talking is easy, action is difficult. *Spanish*
1284. To speak without thinking is to shoot without first taking aim. *Spanish*
1285. A pleasant tongue will lure a snake out of its hole. *Turkish*
1286. Why keep on talking when we know you so well? *West Africa*
1287. A talkative bird will not build a nest. *West Africa*
1288. He who listens, understands. *West Africa*

Superfluity

1289. On a rainy day many offer to water the chickens. *Armenian*
1290. He that is baldheaded has no need of combs. *India*
1291. When one has no needle, thread is of little use. *Japanese*

1292. No fishes are required in a pond which has no wa-
       ter. *Persian*
1293. He who has no room needs no furniture. *Persian*
1294. To make a present to the rich is to throw water into the
       sea. *Russian*
1295. A blacksmith has no need of an axe. *West Africa*

Superiority

1296. He whose virtues exceed his talents is a superior man; he
       whose talents exceed his virtues is an inferior man. *Chinese*
1297. He who watches the chess game in silence is a superior
       man. *Chinese*
1298. Men carry their superiority inside, animals outside. *Russian*

Suspicion

1299. If you would avoid suspicion, don't lace your shoes in a melon
       field. *Chinese*
1300. The melon seller does not cry "bitter melons." *Chinese*
1301. Shake a bridle over a Yorkshireman's grave and he'll rise and
       steal the horse. *English*
1302. When the fox preaches, look to your geese. *German*
1303. Where you hear there are plenty of cherries, always carry a
       small basket. *Greek*
1304. You make a pretense of preserving the hair while you are
       cutting off the head. *India*
1305. Never shave a corpse alone, for fear your hand would slip and
       you'd be accused of murder. *Irish*
1306. Always check that there's bread under the butter. *Irish*
1307. The miller's pigs are fat, but God knows whose grain they
       ate. *Irish*
1308. I know they are all honest men, but my cloak is nowhere to be
       found. *Spanish*

T

After they
had ravished
her she called
out to the
night watchman.

Arab

Teachers
Thrift and Prudence
Timeliness
Travel
Truth and Falsehood

Teachers

1309. A good teacher is better than a barrelful of books. *Chinese*
1310. Teachers open the door, but you must enter by yourself. *Chinese*
1311. Whoever cares to learn will always find a teacher. *German*
1312. With whatever teachers you mingle, such letters you will learn. *Greek*
1313. In every head is a different degree of understanding, and every teacher has a different portion of science. *Hindustan*
1314. Drink water after straining, and adopt a teacher after you know him. *Hindustan*
1315. As is the teacher, so will the scholar be. *India*
1316. If the teacher be corrupt, the world will be corrupt. *Persian*

Thrift and Prudence

1317. A stitch in time saves nine. *English*
1318. Providence provides for the provident. *English*
1319. Although it rains, throw not away your watering pot. *English*
1320. Save at the spigot and let out at the bunghole! *English*
1321. Ask your purse what you should buy. *English*
1322. A blanket is not to be thrown away because of lice. *Hindustan*
1323. Don't throw away your dirty water until you have got clean. *Irish*
1324. A man who always wears his best kimono has no Sunday clothes. *Japanese*
1325. If you have eaten the morsel on Wednesday, do not look for it on Thursday. *Russian*

1326. Buy what you don't need and you'll sell what you can't spare. *Scottish*

1327. May God send water to the well that folks think will never run dry. *Scottish*

1328. The one who saves something has something. *Swedish*

1329. When the soup is boiling over, a ladle is not too costly. *Turkish*

1330. Where there is more than enough, more than enough is wasted. *West Africa*

1331. If you would eat eggs, take care of the hen. *West Africa*

1332. He who does not mend old clothes will not wear new ones. *Yugoslav*

1333. He who buys what he does not need will soon have to sell the things he does. *Yugoslav*

1334. He who works has much; he who saves, still more. *Yugoslav*

1335. If a man does not begin saving while the sack of wheat is full, he will not save when the wheat is at the bottom of the sack. *Yugoslav*

Timeliness

1336. Make your bargain before beginning to plow. *Arab*

1337. After they had ravished her, she called out to the night watchman. *Arab*

1338. Clean the drainpipes while it is still good weather. *Chinese*

1339. When your horse is on the brink of a precipice, it is too late to pull the reins. *Chinese*

1340. Water which is distant is no good for a fire which is near. *Chinese*

1341. Make hay while the sun shines. *English*

1342. Strike while the iron is hot. *English*

1343. The early bird gets the worm. *English*

1344. Never put off until tomorrow what you can do today. *English*

1345. 'Tis not enough to run well, unless you set out in due time. *French*
1346. One "take this" is better than two "thou shalt haves." *French*
1347. He that always thinks it is too soon is sure to come too late. *German*
1348. The wolf that measures the distance goes hungry. *Greek*
1349. Don't ask for watermelon in the middle of winter. *Greek*
1350. Today is, tomorrow is not. *Hindustan*
1351. When the wolf has run off with the child, then the door is made fast. *Hindustan*
1352. Everything must wait its turn . . . peach blossoms for the second month and chrysanthemums for the ninth. *Japanese*
1353. When you're thirsty, it's too late to think about digging a well. *Japanese*
1354. An incident should be remedied before it occurs. *Persian*
1355. By the time you put on your arms, the war is finished. *Persian*
1356. By the time ointment is brought from Iraq, the snakebitten man will die. *Persian*
1357. It is too late to think of the wine when the cask is empty. *Russian*
1358. Time does not bow to you, you must bow to time. *Russian*
1359. After the daughter is married, then we find many would-be sons-in-law. *Russian*
1360. A thing done at a wrong time should be regarded as not done. *Sanskrit*
1361. Little use to repair the tank bung after the water has escaped. *Sanskrit*
1362. The road of by and by leads to the house of never. *Spanish*
1363. What is not done on its day will not be done in a year. *Turkish*

Travel

1364. He that has long legs travels fast. *Arab*

1365. The mile is long to him who is tired. *Japanese*
1366. On a long journey, even a straw weighs heavy. *Spanish*
1367. Who makes frequent inquiries about the road does not go astray. *Yugoslav*

Truth and Falsehood

1368. Always tell the truth in the form of a joke. *Armenian*
1369. Honey in his mouth, knives in his heart. *Chinese*
1370. One man tells a lie, dozens repeat it as the truth. *Chinese*
1371. Honesty is the best policy. *English*
1372. You're an honest man, and I'm your uncle, and that's two lies. *English*
1373. Only truth is beautiful. *French*
1374. Liars need good memories. *French*
1375. A liar isn't believed even when he tells the truth. *German*
1376. Truth ill-timed is as bad as a lie. *German*
1377. When anger blinds the mind, truth disappears. *German*
1378. Truth gives a short answer; lies go roundabout. *German*
1379. Truth creeps not in corners. *German*
1380. A lie becomes true when one believes it. *German*
1381. Truths are not uttered from behind masks. *Greek*
1382. A tongue's slip is a truth's revelation. *Greek*
1383. When a poor man speaks the truth he is not believed. *Greek*
1384. Rogues listen not to discourses on honesty. *India*
1385. There are more lies told at a wake than in a courtroom. *Irish*
1386. A little truth helps the lie go down. *Italian*
1387. Oil and truth will get uppermost at last. *Italian*
1388. The cleverest of lies only lasts a week. *Japanese*
1389. A lie has no legs but scandalous wings. *Japanese*
1390. A truthful wanton is as great a miracle as a square egg. *Japanese*
1391. Truth is straight, but judges are crooked. *Russian*
1392. The wise man says "I am looking for truth," and the fool, "I have found truth." *Russian*

1393.   Bury truth in a golden coffin and it will break it open.   *Russian*

1394.   The dexterous make even untruths appear truths as those skilled in painting can make hollows and eminences on a level surface.   *Sanskrit*

1395.   Do not lie for want of news.   *Scottish*

1396.   If all things are true then that's no lie.   *Scottish*

1397.   He that would speak the truth must have one foot in the stirrup.   *Turkish*

1398.   To listen to a lie is harder than to tell it.   *Turkish*

1399.   The liar's house was burning but no one would believe it.   *Turkish*

1400.   Tell a lie on Saturday and you will be ashamed on Sunday.   *Turkish*

1401.   Truth keeps the hand cleaner than soap.   *West Africa*

1402.   A lie has seven variations, the truth none.   *West Africa*

1403.   Speak the truth, but leave immediately after.   *Yugoslav*

1404.   A lie has short legs.   *Yugoslav*

1405.   The more liars there are, the easier one can determine the truth.   *Yugoslav*

1406.   Truth is dew from heaven, catch it in a clean receptacle.   *Yugoslav*

U

It is of no
use to carry
an umbrella
if your shoes
are leaking.
Irish

Useless Pursuits

Useless Pursuits

1407. The cat, though blind, still hankers after mice. *Arab*
1408. He has no home, but he is looking for the door. *Armenian*
1409. Do not give ruffles to him who wants a shirt. *English*
1410. Music helps not the toothache. *English*
1411. When a man is dead there is no use calling the doctor. *French*
1412. A cat with gloves never catches mice. *Greek*
1413. By throwing dust one cannot conceal the moon. *Hindustan*
1414. You cannot separate water by beating it with a fork. *Hindustan*
1415. There is no twisting a rope of sand. *Hindustan*
1416. It is little use to dig a well after the house has caught on fire. *Hindustan*
1417. No use giving a mirror to a blind man or singing to a deaf man. *India*
1418. A blind man sat behind a pile of stones and thought that nobody could see him. *India*
1419. However much water you may pour over a stone, it will still remain a stone. *India*
1420. Never pour water over a drowned mouse. *Irish*
1421. It's no use carrying an umbrella if your shoes are leaking. *Irish*
1422. It's no use boiling your cabbage twice. *Irish*
1423. He cannot manage the calf and yet he wants to carry the bull. *Italian*
1424. The dog may bay, but still the moon stands steady as before. *Italian*
1425. The cask can yield naught but the wine it contains. *Italian*
1426. If the fiber of the hemp is rotten, you can never make a good rope of it. *Italian*

1427.   One cannot learn to swim in a field.   *Japanese*
1428.   To forgive the unrepentant is like making pictures on water.   *Japanese*
1429.   It is foolish to try to graft a bamboo shoot onto a cherry tree.   *Japanese*
1430.   The house is ruined to its foundation, yet the master thinks of painting the parlor.   *Persian*
1431.   He waters an elephant with a spoon.   *Persian*
1432.   No applause can be made with one hand.   *Persian*
1433.   You cannot hang everything on one nail.   *Russian*
1434.   However early you get up, you cannot hasten the dawn.   *Spanish*
1435.   Do not search for a cat with five feet.   *Spanish*
1436.   After the camp was looted, we watched it for forty days and forty nights.   *Turkish*
1437.   Throwing pebbles at an elephant in no way disturbs him.   *West Africa*
1438.   There is little use building a fence around the garden to keep out the gopher.   *Yugoslav*
1439.   It is easy to throw a stone into the Danube, but rather difficult to get it out.   *Yugoslav*

The man that knows the price of everything knows the value of nothing.

Irish

Value
Vanity

Value

1440. A man's value is that which he sets upon himself.   *French*
1441. The scales tell us what is light and what is heavy, but not what is gold and what is silver.   *German*
1442. Pearls are of no value in a desert.   *Hindustan*
1443. Where a man's talents are not valued is no place for him; what should a washerman do in a place where the people go naked?   *Hindustan*
1444. One does not know the worth of teeth while they last.   *India*
1445. An empty house gives better value to its owner than an owing tenant.   *Irish*
1446. The man that knows the price of everything knows the value of nothing.   *Irish*

Vanity

1447. An eloquent cock crows as soon as it comes out of the egg.   *Arab*
1448. The rooster that crows too long tires his own throat.   *Greek*
1449. The crow, whilst learning to walk like a swan, forgot its own gait.   *Hindustan*
1450. I'd make money if I could buy him for any price and sell him at his own.   *Irish*
1451. He fancies himself so much that his mother is trying to remember were the shepherds looking on when he was born.   *Irish*
1452. He who never boasts is esteemed at a third more than his value, if he is worth anything.   *Italian*
1453. Don't remind a vain man of his pimples.   *Russian*
1454. Self praise smells bad.   *Swedish*

W

If there
were wisdom
in beards,
all goats
would be
prophets.
Armenian

Weeping
Wisdom
Wishful Thinking

Weeping

1455. Weeping washes the face. *Hindustan*
1456. To weep in season is better than to laugh out of season. *Persian*
1457. The man who weeps over the world will cry his eyes out. *Yugoslav*
1458. He who laughs on Friday weeps on Sunday. *Yugoslav*

Wisdom

1459. The eyes are of little use if the mind be blind. *Arab*
1460. See that you are wise, but also learn how to appear ignorant. *Armenian*
1461. If there were wisdom in beards, all goats would be prophets. *Armenian*
1462. Learn to handle a writing brush and you'll never handle a begging bowl. *Chinese*
1463. Learning is weightless, a treasure you can always carry easily. *Chinese*
1464. The wise man forgets insults as the ungrateful forget benefits. *Chinese*
1465. Intelligence consists in recognizing opportunity. *Chinese*
1466. The mind is emperor of the body. *Chinese*
1467. A word to the wise is enough. *English*
1468. He who has imagination without learning has wings but no feet. *French*
1469. What little Hans didn't learn, big Hans doesn't know. *German*
1470. Wisdom is the sunlight of the soul. *German*
1471. Reason is the wise man's master; experience is the fool's. *German*
1472. Wonder is the beginning of wisdom. *Greek*

1473. To say witty things is not always a sign of wisdom. *Greek*

1474. If the body is enslaved, at least the mind is free. *Greek*

1475. Wisdom makes a weak man strong, a poor man king, a good generation of a bad one, and a foolish man reasonable. *Irish*

1476. A questioning man is halfway to being wise. *Irish*

1477. The wise discourses of a poor man go for nothing. *Italian*

1478. He who knows should rule, and he who does not know should obey. *Italian*

1479. A man cannot leave his wisdom or his experience to his heirs. *Italian*

1480. A wise man in a fool's service is a clear pearl thrown into lacquer. *Japanese*

1481. Wise men do not contend against the tongues of fools. *Japanese*

1482. A gourd has a large head but no brains. *Persian*

1483. Once I had the strength but no wisdom, now I have the wisdom but no strength. *Persian*

1484. A wise companion is half the journey. *Russian*

1485. You cannot buy wisdom abroad if there is none at home. *Russian*

1486. Wisdom is born; stupidity is learned. *Russian*

1487. Knowledge is the most precious treasure of all things because it can never be given away nor stolen nor consumed. *Sanskrit*

1488. Fools get things mixed up and wise men straighten them out. *Scottish*

1489. All complain of lack of silver, none complain of lack of wit. *Scottish*

1490. All the wit of the world is not in one head. *Scottish*

1491. No man gains wisdom through his father's experience. *Spanish*

1492. Knowledge is madness if good sense does not direct it. *Spanish*

1493. Even though you know a thousand things, ask the man who knows one. *Turkish*

1494. If wits were put at auction, everyone would buy his own. *Turkish*

1495. Repetition is the mother of knowledge. *West Africa*
1496. Not to know is bad, but not to wish to know is worse. *West Africa*
1497. Man is learning all his life and yet he dies in ignorance. *Yugoslav*

Wishful Thinking

1498. They asked a bullfrog, "Why do you continually croak?" He replied, "I'm enchanted with my voice." *Armenian*
1499. The crow was killed by the storm; he died by my curse, says the owl. *India*
1500. The sparrow flying in the rear of the hawk thinks the hawk is fleeing. *Japanese*